Mastering the Moneyed Mind, Volume I

Mastering the Moneyed Mind, Volume I

The Causes, Culprits, and Context of our Money Troubles

Dr. Christopher Bayer

BEP

BUSINESS EXPERT PRESS

Leader in applied, concise business books

Mastering the Moneyed Mind, Volume I: The Causes, Culprits, and Context of our Money Troubles
Copyright © Business Expert Press, LLC, 2021.

First published in 2021 by
Business Expert Press, LLC
222 East 46th Street, New York, NY 10017
www.businessexpertpress.com

ISBN-13: 978-1-95152-770-9 (paperback)
ISBN-13: 978-1-95152-771-6 (e-book)

Business Expert Press Economics and Public Policy Collection

Collection ISSN: 2163-761x (print)
Collection ISSN: 2163-7628 (electronic)

Cover and interior design by S4Carlisle Publishing Services Private Ltd., Chennai, India

First edition: 2021

10 9 8 7 6 5 4 3 2 1

Printed in the United States of America.

Abstract

The Causes, Culprits, and Context of Our Money Troubles is the first volume of a multi-volume series of books, titled *Mastering the Moneyed Mind, Volume I: The Causes, Culprits, and Context of our Money Troubles*. Each volume in the series is undergirded by critical principles in psychology, neuroeconomics, and finance and offers meaningful strategies that reflect evidence derived from more than 30 years of practice in psychological counseling specific to topics in human behavior and money. The series highlights psychological perspectives on the most prominent money mismanagement and corruption cases in the United States, providing a solid historical context, in Volumes 1 to 4 before centering, in subsequent volumes, on current day, 2020 (and beyond) since issues include, pandemics, stock market crashes, and global social unrest.

This buildup of information from the past to the present offers the reader a historical and economic view of the psychology of money management before offering a denouement of what we are witnessing today with global cries and crises. The reader is invited to accept and acknowledge, in Volumes 1 to 4, the intriguing histories presented through purposefully dated stories, articles, experiences, and realities—the chronological essence that frames the progression of the series.

As the first volume in the series, Volume I presents time-tested evidence on the causes, culprits, and contexts of our money troubles and lays the foundation with definitions for key terminologies discussed in the full series. Filled with tales and exemplifications, readers are introduced, pseudonymously, to sample clients of money–mind imbalances, such as the "11-million-dollar man" who becomes corrupted by money's influence, which unbalances his internal Gyroscope. Prepared, strategically, with the aim of establishing the foundations for transitioning to the remaining volumes in the series, Volume I explores the history of our relationship with money—specifically, the role morality and the concept of "virtue" have played in that history, and the wealth versus money[1] dichotomy.

---

[1]Going back to Aristotle, we redefine wealth as an all-encompassing concept, a holistic idea—its material component being but a part of the whole—without which what we see as "the good life," including happiness and fulfillment, is simply not possible.

The volume centers on the root of the concept of "money" and draws readers to examine past- and present-day corruptions derived from money's influence. Readers are led to examine the concepts and theories from great economists of yore and are presented with the author's (a working psychologist's) analysis of the theories of Adam Smith, Karl Marx, and J.M. Keynes to create a theoretical foundation for the Gyroscope methodology (described in Volume IV) bursting with practical, meaningful solutions for managing psychological issues related to money.

Keywords

psychology; finance; neuroeconomics; behavioral finance; money; morality; Wall Street; increasing consumption; commerce; financial; economics; disbalancing; wealth versus money; corruption; materialism

Table of Contents

Foreword

In *The Causes, Culprits, and Context of our Money Troubles*, Dr. Christopher Bayer, The Wall Street Psychologist, presents a historical context for examining our relationship with money. Built on knowledge and lessons derived from his long research and clinical career, Dr. Bayer introduces the reader to comprehensive information about the historical evolution of money, its role as an engine of growth, and as a key component in any high-functioning, well-adjusted modern person's worldview. His presentation of a psychological understanding of money is apropos and timely, as it draws on historical and contemporary wisdom to exemplify important ideas regarding our relationship with money.

Who is better suited to tell us of the *Causes, Culprits, and Context of Our Money Troubles* than Dr. Bayer who knows the "Street?" His career experience as a psychologist for Wall Street financiers complements his presentations, and offers the readers an interesting, 21st century view of historic problems with money as well as important lessons about the historical, moral, and psychological context for money. Upon this important foundation, readers are led into a step-by-step arrangement of the lessons and potential problems that are derived from the (mis)use of money, which provides a broader context for engaging in meaningful activities that empower them to develop a healthy relationship with money.

Since the early 1980s, he has practiced as a psychologist and psychoanalyst in New York, specializing in the treatment of financial services executives and their families in the securities and banking industries. From the boardroom to the boiler room, his practice spans every stratum of the financial services spectrum, with a case load that touches virtually all of the major banks, securities firms, law practices, and boutique private capital firms on Wall Street. Dr. Bayer has treated nearly a thousand financial executives, brokers, analysts, financial consultants, venture capitalists, financial product developers, Wall Street lawyers, traders, portfolio managers, and entrepreneurs.

Through their eyes, he has witnessed the dramatic evolution, and cyclical implosion, of the financial sector. Over the course of decades, he has leveraged this rare, highly privileged insider perspective to develop unique treatment methods, including The Gyroscope—a prescriptive methodology that offers meaningful, stepwise techniques and strategies for managing real-life problems. Outlined throughout his books, Dr. Bayer's methods also address the causes and effects of the devastating psychological and physiological damage wreaked by these occupations, the dangerous obsessions, the self-destructive lifestyles, the cycles of abuse, the pathological infidelities, and so much more. Dr. Bayer has seen what few see: the physical and personal consequences of our culture's fascination with the pursuit of money and success at all costs. This volume represents the culmination of the decades he has spent alleviating the pain of his clients.

Today, when not treating clients, Dr. Bayer devotes his time to writing, teaching, supervision, and the development of a financial management-training program for young adults transitioning to college (www.money-mind101.com). His efforts are aimed at helping financial services professionals overcome self-destructive behavior and create an inner gyroscope in order to significantly increase the probability of their financial and personal success and happiness. He also counsels early career professionals, helping them avoid the psychological pitfalls that lie ahead. For his clients, the one constant force in their frenetic lives is the dangerous, driving obsession with money. But is it the love of money that is the root of all evil?[2] Or is it the lack of money that is the source of all our ills?[3] This is the historic enigma with which Dr. Bayer and his clients continue to wrestle in treatment. This volume is Dr. Bayer's call to action—a call for you, the reader, to act.

Whether you are just out of college and starting to save (or squander) your first paycheck, a midcareer professional with multiple asset classes and levels of commitment, or someone looking forward to retirement and wanting to make the most of living on a fixed income, Volume I could

---

[2]Paul (1 Timothy, 6:7–10).

[3]G.B. Shaw. *Man and Superman: The Revolutionist's Handbook* (New York, NY: Heritage Press).

help you to (a) see the money to be made and had in a healthy, balanced way, (b) avoid the pitfalls entrapping common man and sophisticated financier alike, and (c) use spending (and nonspending) opportunities as opportunities for growth.

Dr. Anestine Hector-Mason,
Managing Director, The Conscious Press, LLC.

Introduction

We live in a money-mad culture. Fifty-five percent of Americans are investors. Seventy percent of America's assets are controlled by people over 50 ("AARP-ites"). And yet two-thirds of the world's adults are financially illiterate. Kids know next to nothing about money. Money is a tool affording freedom and flexibility to us all and emotional and physical security for many. Money creates autonomy! Making money is extremely exciting and stimulating. Money, mind you, is on everyone's mind. It empowers, creates, unlocks potential. It can build self-esteem, a sense of wholeness, emotional safety, status, and self "net worth." Money, however, must be put into perspective vis-à-vis one's life. Honor, dignity, duty, self-respect, and empathy are human intangibles that generally function and thrive independently of money. Of course, money can always aid and abet, so to speak, but having money can also alleviate stress. These are essential components of the moneyed mind, which the text explores and documents through comprehensive assessment and deep analysis.

Mastering the Moneyed Mind is a result of my studies with financial professionals (FPs), my own history as an investor, my moneymaking projects, money-development philosophy, and money psychology models. Understanding how money and one's mind interact and interweave is essential for financial health, which is just as important as physical or mental health. I created the series to help advance thought in neuroeconomics and behavioral finance and to support teaching and learning in the area of financial literacy at all corporate and educational levels. The series is structured to build on the reader's prior knowledge about the psychology of money, and each volume features critical topics aimed at engaging the reader in a myriad of scientific analyses about the causes of and contexts for money troubles—critical foundations that precede practical techniques and solutions for overcoming unhealthy money-mind habits. Summaries of the latest research in the new field of neuroeconomics and true, fresh-from-the-field tales about money-mind habits are complementary, thought-provoking additions that, intentionally, activate critical thinking and support reader analyses of the value of mastering their own "moneyed" mind.

My belief is that thriving in the financial industry requires a level of commitment that consumes the lives of many professionals; in other words, they become incapable of leaving the office at the office. I have witnessed this reality over the last 30 years and have observed all sides of the inability to achieve work–life balance. Although many FPs are very successful in their climb up the corporate ladder and asset accumulation, experience has shown me that they tend to have trouble in their personal relationships. Clearly, it is difficult to reach an adequate level of fulfillment in life unless *both* sides of the coin (i.e., Personal Life and Profe$$ional Life) are addressed. This series draws attention to the importance of supporting and managing each side; it centers on key strategies for addressing the strengths and needs of both sides.

To exemplify important ideas, I offer readers examples of various personality composites all through the series. With regard to this, it is important for me to note that the wisdom that I present in each of my books is drawn from my own personal life experience and my career in clinical psychology. My personal and career experiences are inextricably tied; as such, it is impossible to speak about the psychology of money without drawing attention to authentic stories in my life, some of which include those of my clients, friends, and family. I recognize the importance of not betraying their trust in me and would like my readers to know that references to any person in my book are anonymized composites of personalities and not actual people.

The strategies in the series are designed to help readers become happier and more successful in the office and beyond. For instance, each strategy is formulated with discussions about (a) how to minimize and control codependency; (b) how to negotiate professional rejection and ingratitude; (c) how to communicate effectively; and (d) how to manage unrealistic expectations. Additionally, readers are offered evidence-based, time-tested techniques on how to reduce stress and feel more satisfied and confident inside and outside of the workplace. In utilizing the innovative and practical strategies and techniques outlined in the book, anyone can learn to be in better control of their inner selves and, in turn, their career or business. In the language of my series, I believe that professionals must create their own universe, one rooted in harmony, well-being, and prosperity. Business success and emotional balance go hand in hand; it is naïve to think otherwise. The power and necessity of emotional and spiritual health can never be underestimated, especially in the demanding, chaotic, and exciting world of today's fast-paced, technology- and innovation-driven markets and industries.

Money, the mind, and the moneyed mind are evergreen subjects that hold an enduring and evolving interest for the vast majority of readers of nonfiction. In the wake of multiple financial scandals and The Great Recession, with real wages stagnating for a generation and the gap between the 99 percent and the 1 percent wider than ever, with assorted billionaires and other ultra-rich more and more in the public eye (e.g., Bloomberg, Romney, Trump) and seeking higher and higher office, it is more important than ever to understand the meaning of this invention we call money, and to define our relationship to it.

Volume I features an overview of the history of money, presents scientific analyses of human behavior, summarizes the latest research in the exciting new field of neuroeconomics, and captures true, fresh-from-the-field tales of battles with (and victory over) unhealthy money-mind habits. Volume I invites readers to consider, for themselves, stories of mass mind control perpetrated by marketing mavens who use insights and principles in behavioral psychology to make rank materialism, manifested in ever-increasing consumption, palatable to the public. The book features a comprehensive set of techniques and exercises taken from Western and Eastern traditions to emphasize the mind–body connection and the importance of improving our emotional balance and peace of mind; in addition it makes a concrete, convincing, and often poignant case for seeing the ancient surrogate of value, which we call money, as a stepping stone on the road to balanced living and true, multifaceted success.

For anyone who wants to succeed monetarily and emotionally in a world riddled with money madness, this is your guidebook and touchstone. More than simply a collection of proven best practices, *Mastering the Moneyed Mind* embodies a 360-degree approach to improving your psychological and physical wellness. I am a psychologist and business consultant based in New York City and have more than 35 years' experience helping patients deal with the issues stemming from their stressful jobs and hourly command over more multiples of money than the average person will see in a lifetime. I have had the opportunity to apply psychological theory to the emotional experience of people on the frontlines of money madness, namely, FPs—the people in the trenches, striving to enrich and protect their clients (and themselves) in a money-mad world.

In writing this book, I have examined data from global and financial history, economic theory, organizational psychology, neuroscience research and literature, stress-management theory and practice, holistic health practices, and, most significantly, from the wealth of ongoing experiences that my patients have, graciously, shared with me over the past three and a half decades. If I can help people sorely tempted by wealth and power—their psyches tested daily, their relationships often off-kilter, their view of the world and people in it warped by a grossly materialistic outlook—I would hope that I can guide someone who is closer to the norm toward an understanding of the crucial role money plays in our lives, and, first and foremost, in our minds.

On Wall Street, the pressure and intensity of the markets wire FPs, spreading them too thin, stressing them, making them tense, high-strung, and therefore fragile. In the rest of corporate America, and in the back offices of small- to medium-sized businesses, the stress and pressure are not much more forgiving. This book, then, is not just a guide to staying healthy while wealthy, but also a psychological survival manual. After all, emotional health underpins financial success. Only when one is centered, emotionally and intellectually, can one master one's universe and truly excel.

For most FPs, self-esteem, self-worth—not just net worth—and a sense of well-being are all pegged to market movement, and, more specifically, hitched to portfolio performance. It is this inherent codependency that financial pros struggle with daily; namely, one's value as a person can become almost entirely dependent on one's production. This is the industry's true occupational hazard—an emotional trap with severe consequences.

And just who are FPs? These soldiers of fortune, thrust mercilessly into the cauldron of temptation, the protagonists whose true-grime (and at times crime) stories color our understanding of the meta-ingredient of our lives known, deceptively, as simply "money"? As a group, they are bright, ambitious, adventurous, lively, libidinous, and mentally invested in accumulating significant wealth. They like making money, they like advising people, and they take pride in growing their clients' portfolios and filling their firms' coffers. At the same time, much of the work they do comes with significant emotional and psychological side effects. Ultimately, the relationship between money and the mind, although most so for denizens of the financial services industry, is serious business for us all. The better we understand money, the more we can benefit from our interaction with it.

CHAPTER 1

The History of Our Relationship with Money

Financial professionals (FPs) earn money by using money; in essence, they use money to make money. This distinction separates FPs from virtually all other occupations. Even a sales professional in another industry, fixated on driving revenue, is still selling a product or a service in order to make money. In the financial services sector, however, the products for sale are financial instruments.

By necessity, the financial services professional develops a more intimate relationship with a more complex concept of money than simply the idea of legal tender. In any field of endeavor aside from philanthropy, money received as compensation for time spent and toil expended is one way to measure aptitude and success. And yet, unlike the architect, the composer, the tradesman, the artist, or the doctor—in whose professions success is also measured by the quality of what is produced or created—too many FPs view money as *the only* benchmark of success.

Still, while the accumulation of wealth needs to be a priority, it need not be the exclusive objective of living and working. Money can be the means to an infinite number of ends and to infinite fulfillment. Sometimes, money can buy happiness, if you know how to spend it the right way and you invest more of yourself in other areas. Sure, FPs have to deal with the curse in disguise of being constantly surrounded by money, but they need not be consumed by an obsession with it. It is key to strike a balance between having a healthy interest in money yet understanding how to use resources to produce professional *and* personal fulfillment. This is the philosophical cornerstone of the Gyroscope methodology. Greed can be good, but only if you know how to channel the fruits of your labor to nurture true fulfillment. Greed by itself consumes. There is a fine line between greed and money lust, and brutal work ethic on a level playing field.

To flourish in this complex industry and get beyond the cash-grabbing herd mentality, you need to understand—or perhaps *reconceptualize* is the word—the psychology of money. To do that, you first need to map the trajectory of how our relationship with money has historically evolved within the confines of our culture. It was the noted philosopher and essayist George Santayana who first uttered the now oft-misquoted phrase "Those who cannot remember the past are condemned to repeat it," sometimes called *Santayana's Law of Repetitive Consequences*.[1] Perhaps in no industry, with its cyclicality of scandals and market implosions, is Santayana's cliché more relevant than it is in finance. This section plots that course, from ancient rudimentary forms of commerce through the highly nuanced offerings of Wall Street.

We start with *The Origins of the Money–Mind Collective*, which establishes the symbiotic relationship between the mind and money, from the earliest utilization of currency as a method of exchanging value. Subsequently, we explore *The Psychology behind the Evolution of Commerce*, which charts a course through the history of money, banking, and the markets. This is not a simple historical review but an examination of the psychological components of milestones in the development of money as a system of assessing and exchanging value. We then fast-forward to *The Century of the Self* and a remarkable documentary, produced by Adam Curtis, extrapolating on his observations of how the theories of Freud related to the self are now applied to techniques of influencing mass-consumerism, narcissism, and artificial self-esteem systems.

As we proceed, in *This Is How We Do Things Here* and in *Would You Put Your Mother in It?* we narrow our range further to explore Wall Street culture. With *The Right Tools in the Wrong Hands*, I present a cautionary tale reflecting on what can go terribly wrong when you do not have a fundamental appreciation of the development of the psychology of money. Finally, *The Banality of Corruption* explores the systemic acceptance of a

---

[1] G. Santayana. 1905. *Life of Reason. Reason in Common Sense*, Vol. 1 (New York, NY: Charles Scribner's Sons), p. 284.

warped version of what the Street has become, and other relevant subjects. Through this awareness, you, the reader, might not necessarily repeat the mistakes that so many so often have made.

Our money, our minds, and our morality have been interwoven since the very first transaction exchanging value was consummated. For some reason, when it comes to discussing the history of commerce and finance, historians tend to strip out the psychology and morality, rarely straying far from the cold hard facts. Psychology tends to be considered only when exploring aspects of marketing, trend analysis, and product development, but usually to illustrate some sort of Jedi mind trick or explain how someone had diabolically exploited some herd-mentality quirk of humanity. Rarely do we see much in the way of a proper analysis of our psychological relationship to money, probably because it is such a frustratingly complex subject.

We may have made impressive advances in our studies of the inner workings of this wondrous machine we call the mind—mind-boggling advances, one might say—but what we do not know about its mechanics far outweighs the facts we have firmly in hand. Ultimately, in our Economics classes, business schools, financial fora, and in the business media, it is much easier to explore the mechanics of money, regurgitate facts, and debate trends related to specific market cycles than it is to unwind the intricacies of the psychological drivers within Street personnel.

At cocktail or dinner parties, in bars and restaurants, there is discussion of such lemming-like phenomena as a run on a stock or mass anxiety motivating a panic during a downturn, but rarely does the conversation delve deeply into the relationship between the mind and money. The reality is that the remarkable cyclicality of market trends, spanning hundreds, if not thousands, of bubbles and bursts across all borders simply would not exist without the psychological underpinnings—without the idiosyncrasies—of human behavior.

You see, when it comes to understanding the historical significance of money to humanity, it really is that much easier to simply focus on the who, what, where, when, and how than to invest the time to truly capture the why. Examining the history of money through the lens of a psychologist, however, will enable you begin developing a new awareness of why we do what we do when it comes to money.

The Source and Evolution of Money

Any discussion on the psychology of money starts with the etymology of the word, and a quick search on the Internet is bound to bring forth numerous valuable definitions, such as the following:

> Money is anything that is generally accepted as payment for goods and services and repayment of debts. The main functions of money are distinguished as: a medium of exchange, a unit of account, a store of value, and occasionally, a standard of deferred payment. (McCumiskey 2011)

I find Wikipedia to be a valuable source of collaboratively developed information and add the following information about money from that source as well:

> Nearly all contemporary money systems are based on fiat money. Fiat money is without value as a physical commodity, and derives its value by being declared by a government to be legal tender; that is, it must be accepted as a form of payment within the bound-aries of the country, for "all debts, public and private". By law, the refusal of an offer to pay in legal tender extinguishes the debt in the same way acceptance does. (https://en.wikipedia.org/wiki/Money)

By this definition, one can take money to represent the psychological *glue* that has always fueled commerce, facilitating and creating civiliza-tion as we know it today. Surely, without a medium to enable commerce, there is no viable way to establish and maintain the complex network of relationships that comprise the idea of "community."

The term "money" is believed to have originated with the Roman temple of Juno Moneta, which also served as the ancient capital's mint[2] (see D'Eprio and Pinkowish 1998). Therefore, in the collective conscious-ness, The Coin of Juno was the cultural entity from which all commercial relationships, aside from familial relationships and friendships, derived.

---

[2] P. D'Eprio and M.D. Pinkowish. 1998. *What Are the Seven Wonders of the World?* (New York, NY: First Anchor Books), p. 192. ISBN 0-385-49062-3.

Some Slang Terms for Money

How Many Do You Know?

Bank, bank rags, beans, Benjamin, benji, big faces, big ones, bill, bone, boodle, bread, bucks, cabbage, cash, cheese, cheddar, chips, clams, coin, c-note, dead presidents, deuce, dosh, double sawbuck, dough, ducats, fin, fiver, five-spot, folding stuff, faux Euro, Franklin, geld, green, greenback, Hamilton, hay, Jackson, Jefferson, ka-ching, lettuce, lolly, (filthy) lucre, moolah, paint, paper, readies, rocks, sawbuck, scratch, smackers, spondoolies, shekels, tenner, ten-spot, twenty-spot, wonga, wood, and yard.

Certainly, the system of commerce was still heavily dependent on local barter, but the minting of money represented the advancement of a culture, especially with regard to economic activities within a culture. In a society where religion and government were intertwined to such an extent, having the mint located in a house of worship reinforced the authority of the emerging system of value exchange.

The Evolution of Money

The Psychological History of Change

12000 BC: In China, cowry shells become the first medium of exchange, or money.

9000 BC: Livestock is used as a form of exchange.

5000 BC: Metal objects are introduced as money.

5000 BC: A non-Semitic nation, likely of Indian origin, establishes trade routes between Asia Minor and the Far East.

2500 BC: The ancient Babylonians establish a complex system of lending, borrowing, and holding money on deposit, providing letters of credit.

1800 BC: Usury, the lending of money with a charge of added interest, is practiced by the Sumerians and Greeks.

700 BC: The Lydians are the first in the Western world to make coins.

118 BC: Banknotes in the form of leather money are used in China.

200 AD: During the reign of Augustus, there are numerous references to the deposit and withdrawal of money from banks and the writing of "orders" to withdraw funds, make transfers between accounts, take out loans, and pay brokerage fees.

325: The Council of Nicaea issues a prohibition on lending money (by clerics) at interest.

500s: Paper money originates in Europe during the Middle Ages.

960: The issuance of the earliest known paper money in China.

1157: Private banks are recorded as having existed in Venice as early as 1157. These are primarily banking entities that serve the government.

1204: Following the Sack of Constantinople, the goldsmiths of Lombardi (Italy) become especially influential in financial circles, establishing banks in Delft (the Netherlands) and Calais (France).

1300s: Muslims in the Islamic Empire are forbidden by the Koran to engage in usury, so banks partner with businesses rather than lending them money.

1530s: Strings of beads made from clam shells, called wampum, are used by North American Indians as money.

1550s: John Calvin, a Swiss theologian, develops a more sophisticated understanding of usury. Canon law banned the lending of money at interest, but Calvin felt that loans for business development were sound; heretofore, loans to the poor had been forbidden.

1584: Banco di Rialto, the first public bank in Europe, is founded in Venice by acts of the Senate.

1685: The French Colonial Government in Canada, suffering from a lack of francs, begins issuing money printed on pasteboards from the standard playing deck of the time.

1773: The London Stock Exchange has its humble beginnings in the trading of shares at New Jonathan's, a London coffeehouse and the first building ever to be known as a stock exchange.

1776: The First Continental Congress issues $80 million of 6 percent government bonds in order to finance the war.

1781: The Bank of North America is established in Philadelphia.

1784: Shares in the Bank of New York are first sold.

1791: The First Bank of the United States is chartered.

1780: During the American Revolution, inflation is so great that the price of corn rises 10,000 percent, the price of wheat 14,000 percent, the price of flour 15,000 percent, and the price of beef 33,000 percent.

1792: A group of 24 brokers sign an agreement to meet at regular hours daily under an old buttonwood tree on Wall Street, in Lower Manhattan, New York City, to buy and sell securities.

1794: The first coin minted in the United States is a silver dollar, issued on October 15, 1794.

1816: England makes gold a benchmark of value.

1817: The first formal constitution of the NYSE Board is adopted.

1862: The first U.S. paper money is issued.

1910: A group of leading industrialists, bankers, and financiers meet in secret on Jekyll Island, off the coast of Brunswick, Georgia, to create a "scientific currency" for the United States. The attendees, including J.P. Morgan, Joseph Pulitzer, William K. Vanderbilt, Henry Goodyear, Cyrus McCormick, Herbert Lehman, and Bernard Baruch, form The Fed.

1913: The Federal Reserve Act of 1913 positions the United States as the leading source of world financial power.

1930: The gold standard is abandoned in the wake of the Great Depression.

1950: Diners Club issues the first credit card.

Today: One-fourth of the world's population lives on less than $500 per year.

How Money Defines Our Identity

Perhaps more so than anything else in our culture, the concept of money is a most consistent, persistent source of self-identification. For the majority of people, money represents freedom, as it always has, simply because money provides the resources to facilitate a myriad pursuit. If you do not like your job yet do not have enough money to quit and pursue something else you feel trapped. If you do have enough money to take the leap toward pursuing a more fulfilling occupation, money can be liberating.

Money can buy you the time to try your hand at becoming an artist or a musician, a stay-at-home parent, or an entrepreneur. Money gives us autonomy. If we have enough of it not to be reliant on other people's financial support, then we can be more confident that our decision making and our way in this world are independent. Money can give us a sense of well-being, power, superiority, emotional stability, and, to an extent, inner peace. It can also give us the flexibility to choose how, where, with whom, and at what level of comfort we live our lives. Today, earning and spending our money as we see fit are rights we enjoy as participants in the free market of a democratic society. Still, it was not always this way.

In ancient Greece, wealth was measured in the form of property and land, which was in the hands of the aristocracy. Land and power were inseparable. The aristocracy believed in a closed society, in which the best (aristos) people embraced tradition and conservatism, rejecting meritocracy as too radical. Anyone who would transcend his birthright by acquiring more wealth (and thus more value) merely by working hard was seen as too great a threat to the aristocracy's power.

If a person's intelligence and abilities, rather than his ancestry or feudal status, would have been the more acceptable measure of power and success, then every man could become a kind of king, and a very wealthy one at that. This concept of a meritocracy was quite threatening to the "powers that be." Therefore, money, in the commodity sense, in the form of landholdings, was a powerful psychological tool for stratifying society.

In the Middle of the Night, When We Are All Alone

As part of my practice, I frequently revisit these ancient concepts of morality and virtue with my clients. These are the intrinsic elements of a person's value system. Only by honestly pursuing and attaining virtue can people address their demons. Some of us have a longer road than others to travel. Some of us are psychologically besieged by our own lack of morality yet do not apprehend the source of our misery. To illustrate: I had a client, a top-producing broker for a major Wall Street firm, who was beset by frequent nightmares that were so terrible they drove him into treatment. His deepest, darkest fear? *Poverty.*

Here was a man who was very, very far from being poor. Yet, as time went by, my client would have dreams with the same recurring theme, dreams that grew in frequency and complexity, in which he turned into Oliver Twist, trapped in Fagin's world. This man was all too familiar with the subject. Having grown up in a small, one-bedroom, tenement-style apartment, he *had* come from an impoverished background. He was no longer destitute; still, his psyche was subjecting him to irrational delusions of poverty, and he was terrified. He would have to calm himself by checking on his portfolio. He needed constant reassurance of his ability to survive. Survival he measured only in monetary terms. In effect his money owned his soul.

Progressing through therapy, we eventually discovered that he did some things he wasn't proud of. Riddled with shame and fear, finally engaging in self-reflection and a life review, he was in anguish. Raised as a strict religious person, on some level he genuinely feared that he would be going straight to hell upon his demise.

The client's anxiety levels spiked after the Oliver Twist/Fagin nightmares. His growing net worth did little to soothe his damaged soul. With intensive treatment, he was able to modulate his fear and create a template for making amends. He started focusing on areas of his interest and passion. It was only after he came to terms with key components of the idea of morality that he was able to map out a trajectory of improvement.

The Psychology of Commerce

Consider the following statement:

> The national budget must be balanced. The public debt must be reduced; the arrogance of the authorities must be moderated and controlled. Payments to foreign governments must be reduced if the nation doesn't want to go bankrupt. People must again learn to work, instead of living on public assistance.

Would you hazard a guess at when this warning was uttered and by whom? This statement was made over 2,000 years ago by Roman author, orator, and politician Cicero, in 55 BC. Economic history has a habit of repeating itself, because money—or at least the necessity of gauging value by a tangible means of exchange—is embedded in our DNA.

A statement such as Cicero's could easily be attributed to any number of modern-day politicians or pundits. What is important is that, whether it is Cicero or Fox News, regardless of when such statements are made, they reflect a distinct psychological component to our perception of the collective economic state. Here, Cicero offers an alarmist's view that plays on the insecurities of the populace. One wonders if there was an ancient liberal-leaning opponent who countered Cicero but whose words are lost to us. Looking at the history of finance through a psychological lens can provide the FP with a better understanding of why markets behave the way they do.

Knowledge of Money Is Power

Knowing the origins and understanding the trajectory of one's industry not only adds meaning to one's professional life, but it also impresses clients. Awareness of economic history leads to a better understanding of market trends—a better awareness of what products sell and what people need. Clients prefer interesting bankers, brokers, money managers. It is not always just about the money for clients. They want someone with a pulse; someone with a heart and brain; someone they can get to know, respect, and trust. Boring never inspires.

Knowing what has been leads to a better grasp of what could be, even what will be. Indeed, the ability to predict events, whether rooted in science or mysticism, is an important skill for an FP to have. Clients actually want to admire, respect, and be in awe of their FP. You just have to give them the chance to do it. So, let us dive in.

A Selective History of Our Relationship with Money

To truly understand the symbiotic connection between money and the mind, it is essential to know whence it came and how it developed and persisted as an integral component of the human experience. We won't be delving too deeply into a comprehensive history of commerce. Instead, allow me to present my interpretation of key events, highlighting what I feel are relevant psychological milestones. My experience shows that today's FP needs a grounding in such a psychological history of money, and it is not only the actual milestones but also what these momentous developments have meant to our culture that warrant reflection. With each milestone, consider the impact on the collective consciousness. The evolution of commerce and banking was not simply a product of the evolution of humanity, but rather the central facilitator of progress.

It is an ugly, cruel history, marked by inhumanity, greed, exploitation, violence, death, and destruction. Nonetheless, it is our history. And virtually every thread woven into this grand tapestry has in some manner, either directly or indirectly, influenced all of us today. When contemplating each milestone I provide, I ask you to consider how these developments dramatically altered everyday life.

Money has always been the main engine of civilization's growth and progress. Tracing its trajectory globally, we see that banking practices originally began in Asia; spread to Europe and then to the Americas, Australia, and Africa; and eventually reached even the most remote places in the world. The development of cohesive societies varied greatly in different parts of the world, but it had at least one denominator in common—some form of money to facilitate commercial relationships. Now, let us explore select money-specific developments throughout history and ascertain their psychological ramifications.

The Stigma of Usury

Consider the concept of moneylending, perhaps the greatest engine of growth ever conceived. As far back as the ancient Sumerians and Greeks, the borrowing of goods in exchange for a return enhanced by a premium was practiced. People lent each other cows that were given back after the birthing season along with a new calf. In fact, the word for interest and calf was the same in these ancient cultures. The ancient Babylonians, for instance, were bringing up the charging of excessive interest rates when making loans to the poor as early as 1800 BC.

At the same time many cultures, especially theocracies guided by religious leaders, prohibited the practice of benefiting through the charging of interest. Convening in 325 AD, the First Council of Nicaea forbade clergy to engage in usury, which at the time meant receiving interest of any kind, while the canon merely forbade the clergy to lend money at interest of over 1 percent monthly. Later, ecumenical councils applied this regulation to the laity.

It would take centuries for such prohibitions to be relaxed; at the same time, the collective conscious became etched with the image of the avaricious moneylender. Here was an individual who produced no physical commodities and provided no service beyond trading in the provision of credit. For a culture with no checking accounts or credit cards, in which you were measured according to your ability to produce something of tangible value, the business of making money through lending was seen in a bad light.

The Consolidation of Wealth and Power

In the 1500s and early 1600s, exchange banks were formed in the Netherlands and in parts of Italy to provide currency exchange, made necessary by expanding international trade. Privately owned financial institutions developed alongside state-owned banks. The great banking families of the 1600s and 1700s emerged in Europe: the de' Medicis, the Fuggers, the Rothschilds.

When you study these families, you see they that they were very effective in leveraging their wealth to control entire populations. They wielded enormous power, dominating all aspects of culture, through cooperation or coercion, and were revered as well as feared for the power with which their money endowed them.

This model created even greater systems of commerce, with even larger footprints to facilitate power and control on a regional and eventually a global scale.

The Emergence of Stock Trading

In 1801, the London Stock Exchange was formally instituted, with 550 subscribers and 100 clerks. Stocks were known as funds allocated by a company or the government from its capital for the purposes of financial investment. This was quite a radical concept, as it was able to distribute value in a way that was previously impossible, and provided an even more robust means for the economy's growth.

Shares became known as equal parts into which a company's stocks were divided for their purchase by an individual or another company, who then became a shareholder and was entitled to a proportion of the company's profits. Common shares became known as equities.

The Prominence of Wall Street in Our Culture

Money has also always been a component of man's proclivity for waging war on his fellow man. As the expenses of waging the Revolutionary War grew, banks' shares plus treasury bonds issued under Alexander Hamilton were utilized to finance the war debts of the Continental Congress and the Colonies. As a result, a supply of securities was created, and the first securities exchange—the precursor to the New York Stock Exchange—was formed in Philadelphia in 1790.

This brings us to Wall Street, so named because it ran along a wall that had been built by the Dutch to fortify New Amsterdam. In those times, Wall Street was also a popular place to buy and sell furs, tobacco, spices, molasses, and gunpowder. It has come to symbolize so much more, becoming the epicenter of global finance and, for our purposes, the crux of the relationship between money and the mind.

The fledgling stock exchange grew to meet the needs of buyers and sellers of certain commodities to keep in close contact with each other. The sellers wanted to convert securities into money, and the buyers wanted to purchase particular securities. Interestingly, at first, securities represented money loaned to governments. It was only in the 19th century, with the rise of American business corporations, that commercial securities came to dominate the volume of business transacted.

It costs more today to buy a new car in the United States than it cost Christopher Columbus to equip and undertake three voyages to and from the New World. In 1776, a man who made $4,000 a year was considered very wealthy. A worker earning $5,000 per year in 1978 would be making an adjusted equivalent of nearly $5,000 an hour in 2078. In 1914, the first year income tax was collected, Americans paid a per capita tax of 41 cents, and only 1 percent of the population was obligated to pay taxes at all. Of course, one needs to account for inflation and use a common reference by converting to equivalent standard, but think of what this all means.

I hope this brief history lesson has served to inform you of market development sufficiently to give you a better understanding of why we are the way we are and do the things we do.

The Century of the Self

We consume. Sustenance. Resources. Ideas. Emotions. Each other. Ourselves. We consume. We are ravenous. Consumption is the engine that powers human experience. Consumers drive 70 percent of the U.S. economy; they are essential, they are indispensable. Understanding the psychology fueling our intricate ecosystems of consumption is critical not only to a financial professional's success, but also to his sanity.

Consumption or lack thereof happens for very specific reasons. Drill down deep enough, and you will see that market data is essentially research on consumption patterns, which is ultimately driven by human behavior. Therefore, understanding the psychology of consumption and the ways in which perceptions of consumption are disseminated and manipulated will make the FP more sophisticated in many ways.

There is much more to market dynamics than the law of supply and demand. When you gain the ability to analyze and interpret data through the lens of psychology, you begin to get glimpses of the hidden agendas of the sources of information, whether these be governments, ratings agencies, individuals, public relations officers, corporations, or any number of industry machinators. To consume, or to be consumed? That is the question.

The Psychology of Consumerism Emerges

In 2002, filmmaker Adam Curtis created a remarkable documentary series called The Century of the Self, dissecting the rise of consumerism, the mechanisms of influence, and the manipulation of consumer behavior.[3] Interspersing archival footage with commentary and fact, Curtis explored the application of Freudian theory, specifically the exploitation of the self, not as a vehicle of liberation, but as a tool of manipulation wielded by marketers and politicos to power mass consumerism.

Essentially, by developing techniques to explore the subconscious, Freud unleashed methods that could be applied to mine the hidden recesses of the minds of the masses. His important body of work has today been turned into the basis of entire fields of mass influence—some would say manipulation—positioned to create endless versions of market-controlled happiness, based on how people see and value themselves and others.

The Century of the Self is an extrapolation of the theories of Sigmund Freud, the founder of psychoanalysis, focusing on the way in which public relations experts and politicians have leveraged Freud's theories for the engineering of consent, among other constructs, in order to control and influence opinion. Extrapolating this conversation to another arena, there are several Freudian theories that can be directly applied to the FP's world.

By viewing this documentary and delving deeper into Freudian theory, FPs would better understand how materialism and consumerism interact and ultimately impact financial decision making and client management. Grasping the psychology behind influence can be a useful tool in the savvy FP's tool kit.

Conservatism and conformity were the standards for Western culture in the early to mid-20th century. Then marketers and politicians began

---

[3]A. Curtis. 2002. "The Century of the Self," British Broadcasting Corporation, 240 minutes.

to understand that it was actually individualism, the personal quest for a unique identity, which resonated much more effectively with the consumer or voter.

Curtis explains how politicians on the left, in both Britain and America, perfected techniques developed by business to tap into the internal desires of the self. By gaining a glimpse into these desires, politicians could modify messages to make them much more digestible for mass consumption. Thus psychoanalytical practice was made to serve politics, and the modern focus group was born.

Applying Psychology to Gain an Advantage

Businesses would run marketing campaigns designed to entice consumers to want things they did not necessarily need by surreptitiously aligning their products with such unconscious desires as status, being sexy and desirable, self-esteem, prestige, being superior and better than others, possessing a healthy overall sense of worth and well-being, being a member of the 'in' group, being adored and admired, and being popular.

What has followed since has been an endless parade of celebrity endorsements, PR chicanery, stunt-selling, sexual innuendo, and more, all with the intention of extending to the consumer an inclusion in the illusion of happiness and status via association.

The series goes on to explore the massive marketing potential of not only desire, but also of fear. Deep within all of us lie animalistic instincts that need to be harnessed, controlled. When they are not, we arrive at disasters of the sort visited upon humanity by Nazi Germany. Fear is indeed a powerful motivator, and it can be manipulated to yield results on both sides of the spectrum. Curtis explores how the U.S. government manipulated the citizens' sense of fear to repress our natural, subconscious savage instincts, preserve democracy, and prevent the self-annihilation of our race.

The series then goes on to cover the backlash against this tendency toward mind control that occurred in the 1960s, when a radical group of psychotherapists challenged the influence of Freudian theories. They were inspired by the ideas of Wilhelm Reich, a pupil of Freud's, who advocated that the inner self did not need to be repressed or controlled but rather needed to be encouraged to express itself.

Out of this came a political movement that sought to create new beings, free of the conformity that had been implanted in people's minds by businesses and politicians. The series shows how this trend spread rapidly in America through self-help movement systems like Werner Erhard's Erhard Seminar Training (EST), culminating in the inexorable rise of the expressive self, the "me" generation.

Ever adaptable and ready to seek out new ways of making money, American corporations soon realized that this new self was less of a threat and more of their greatest opportunity so far. It was in their interest to encourage people to feel that they were unique individuals and then exploit this by marketing to them ways to express that individuality. To do this, they turned to techniques developed by Freudian psychoanalysts, aimed at reading the inner desires of the new self.

The final episode of this four-part series explores how politicians on the left, in both Britain and America, turned to the techniques developed by business to read and fulfill the inner desires of the self. Out of this grew a new culture of public relations and marketing in politics, business, and journalism. One of its stars in Britain was Matthew Freud, who followed in the footsteps of Edward Bernays, who essentially invented public relations in the 1920s.

Politicians believed they were creating a new and better form of democracy, one that truly reacted to the inner feelings of the individual. What they didn't realize was that the aim of those who had originally created these techniques had been not to liberate the people but to develop new ways of controlling them.

I highly recommend that FPs view this seminal series, for it really captures the historical development of what today is the basis for how we market and message to consumers. Freud uncovered the importance of the self and, through his exploration, unlocked the way into the mass mind. A better understanding of this can only help you unlock the secrets of the markets, and your client base.

"This Is How We Do Things Here"

The questionable behavior revealed by my clients never ceases to amaze me, nor do the outrageous justifications they nonchalantly tout when explaining away their deeds. For instance, during the past 25 years, I have worked with dozens of financial analysts: sector analysts, mergers and acquisitions (M&A) analysts, hedge fund analysts, and mutual fund analysts. Many of them alleged that they had known cases where peers shared inside/confidential/sensitive information with close family and select friends so that they could buy positions and make killings on these purchases. These are credentialed, trained, highly experienced professionals, who know better. I can only assume that their confessions are honest, although it was unclear to me whether or not they were referring to themselves.

It is important to note here that I've heard stories of some financial analysts taking pride in their illicit behavior, such as one person, overheard to brazenly tout himself as a "Master Thief," describing to everyone who listened to the raw details of how he was able to set up an offshore corporation and subsequently trade through a friend's sister who happened to be his girlfriend's archenemy. There were even stories about strategically timing trades and/or delaying them for microseconds in order to maximize profits and minimize losses, based on inside information. Even if these stories are only locker-room boasts, it still tells us about the appearance of unethical issues in the industry.

Some of the stories on Wall Street relate to illegal practices, specifically, banned by Securities & Exchange Commission regulations. Why do financial analysts go around sharing illegal conduct and behaviors with others? I am sure it had to do with their need to make an impression. It's certainly a textbook characteristic of narcissism—this needs to astonish and astound for the purpose of enhancing one's self-validation, in order to feel worthy and superior. This phenomenon forms the psychological underpinning of what's known as the "Big Swinging Dick" syndrome so prevalent on the Street.

Many of these clients shared a grandiose sense of entitlement, as well as a thrill for screwing the system, their companies, and their clients. Equally disturbing (and intriguing, from the perspective of a psychoanalyst) was a common denominator that threaded its way through thousands of sessions, hundreds of clients: too many of them utterly lacked the capacity to express sincere remorse, guilt, or shame. Many did express these emotions, and they were admirable, even heroic. Some, unfortunately, did not or simply could not.

As a point of disclosure, the majority of my clients have not been financial psychopaths. For the most part, they are psychologically stable people overwhelmed by the extreme pressures they face in a highly demanding work environment. The enormity and terror of the pressure can never be minimized. One client would not go home but would sleep under his desk and work through the night in order to make up for his losses the day before. He would also live much beyond his means as a way of stimulating his production. He thrived on the roller coaster until he was tamed by psychotropic medications, by a crash course I conducted in sleep hygiene, and by an interest in building his Gyroscope.

Still, enough of my clients assumed little responsibility for their actions, because, from their perspective, these dirty little secrets were, in fact, the status quo. A classic refrain went: If the CEOs can do it, why can't we?

Systemic Justification for Corruption

This blind collusion, aka mutual guarantee, aka code of silence, aka omertà, as well as refusal to assume any sort of responsibility for one's behavior, is rooted in a concept known as System Justification Theory, which refers to a social–psychological propensity to support the status quo, often contrary to logic.[4]

This is a fascinating dynamic. You have a large number of members of an industry who not only look the other way, but also endorse this unwritten code of collusion. In any other context, they would likely disparage theft and deception; indeed, many may not actually be personally involved in such practices, or perhaps at least not on a regular basis. Still, there is a collective sense of subconscious acceptance, akin to the police officer who would not inform on a colleague, or even a taxpayer who cheats regularly on his filings.

The corruption has become so systemic as to now be institutionalized— a way of doing business, a fact of life. The way to justify one's actions in a system like this, and to dismiss critics who do not understand

---

[4]J.T. Jost and O. Hunyady. 2002. "The Psychology of System Justification and the Palliative Function of Ideology," *European Review of Social Psychology* 13, pp. 111–53.

the culture, is to say that oft-heard byword of corruption: "this is how we do things here." There is a thread of ego-justification here that is fed by the group dynamic—not guilt by association but the lack of guilt by association.

> System Justification Theory differs from the status quo bias in that it is predominantly motivational rather than cognitive. Generally, the status quo bias refers to a tendency to prefer the default or established option when making choices. In contrast, system justification posits that people need and want to see prevailing social systems as fair and just. The motivational component of system justification means that its effects are exacerbated when people are under psychological threat or when they feel their outcomes are especially dependent on the system being justified.

This collective justification underscores the importance of individualism as an essential tenet of The Wall Street Psychologist's Gyroscope, but within the complexity of the corporate structure. The true bottom line is that you must be true to yourself.

Tacit Approval from Higher Powers

Whatever your beliefs on the subject, it seems safe to say that in the cutthroat world of financial management there often seems to be a greater force at work, pulling strings behind the scenes, while many employees on the ground sweat day after day about bottom lines, profitability, liquidity, and balance sheets. This is perhaps the most common working model for FPs today: the one in which the individual has his own business group within a massive corporate structure that, in some ways, is not transparent. The corporation receives the lion's share of the individual's production credits, usually anywhere from 30 to 70 percent, particularly for old-line firms. FPs frequently broker their own deals with their managers and their firms.

Sometimes, the company serving as an umbrella organization to the individual's enterprise appears benign yet isn't; sometimes upper management and the inner circle have their own agendas, which they promote and pursue via selfish and at times deceptive dealings. They frequently and mercilessly push company products where the fee/commission/split is larger and more lucrative; and, of course, the manager takes home a percentage of his staff's production. Sometimes compensation packages are revamped in a way that dramatically limits the FP's share of his own production. Often, employees are asked to push company-based products—something that may not be in the interest of the employee's business or in the clients' genuine interest.

Disingenuous or even downright corrupt behavior exists on the Street, and yet these dealings are often justified with nothing more than a "Sorry. This is how we do things here."

A Common Scenario

Imagine, for example, that you are a retail stockbroker, having worked as a financial consultant for the same firm for 25 years. You've seen a variety of managers come and go, and by now you are familiar with the old boys' network. You have been an average performer (third or fourth quintile); you make a decent living; you have the golden handcuffs (the great bulk of your retirement funding is placed in your firm's stock), and then along comes a meltdown like the one of 2008 to 2009, and your company's share value plummets by nearly 70 percent.

Meanwhile, the company's new CEO has been on a shopping spree, redecorating his office with furnishings fit for a king. In the broker community, John Thain, Merrill's ousted CEO, is fondly remembered for the $1.2-million office refurbishment bill he left behind, featuring, quite symbolically, a $35,000 office commode. So what is the net result?

Your company's stock is worth pennies of the dollar you were counting on. Your 401K has shrunk more dramatically than a Wall Street CEO from his responsibilities in the wake of the crisis you are all weathering. Upper management continues to take huge bonuses for questionable performances (too many credit-default swaps and mortgage-backed security products), and now the markets are in free fall. Century-old, previously venerable companies are going out of business, and your clients are beating the hell out of you. Where, in all this, is the CEO's fiduciary and moral responsibility to you, the financial consultant?

You feel that you have been forced to work in a deceptive, hostile environment. You feel that you have been betrayed. Your neurotransmitters are in an uproar, you cannot sleep, you are overdrinking and self-medicating, and you are chronically anxious. You are alienated from your spouse, distant from your kids, and literally terrified about the security of your financial future. In times like these, sales of selective serotonin reuptake inhibitors (SSRIs; Prozac, Zoloft, and Lexapro) soar and Big Pharma has a field day.

Again, "this is how we do things here."

Survival Based on Deception

I advise my clients to read General Sun Tzu's "The Art of War." "Every battle is won before it is ever fought" is one of its most enduring and popular adages. To some of us, this may sound like an overly militant approach to financial management, but nevertheless, becoming familiar with a few highlights of Sun Tzu's military treatise (written in China, circa Vth century BC) can help brokers understand the mindset of many higher-ups for whom they toil.

Sun Tzu believed that all war was based on deception, and that the mission was to defeat the enemy psychologically before the battle, breaking his will to fight. Being aware of this tactic—and the fact that, at times, people may use it to get what they want out of you—can help immensely when dealing with one's colleagues, managers, and even clients. If you know that "this is how we do things here" and set the limits of your game, you achieve greater strategic clarity, and feel greater calm, because you are prepared. You empower yourself to plan your trajectory more effectively and, in turn, to complete your mission.

With respect to corporate agendas, it is often helpful to ask yourself: "What is the 'real' (manifest) agenda?" And then: "What is the hidden (latent) one?" Sun Tzu recognized that strategic positioning requires an analysis of both objective and subjective variables. FPs deal with technical trends as well as with sentiment. Both factors are crucial components of decision making. The way in which an FP (for instance) positions trades follows from an assessment of the interaction of trends and emotions that he or she observes.

Sun Tzu believed that effective strategy assumes effecting appropriate, quick responses to chaotic and changing conditions. Professional traders certainly understand Sun Tzu's thinking in this regard. A broker can have a set template, but when market free fall is triggered, he must be able to institute immediate hedging and risk-management contingency actions. In another sense, all the planning and book/technical knowledge in the world can go out the window when a selling craze crashes the market. At these junctures, you have got to have the courage, instincts, and where-withal to act and survive come hell or high water.

Excellent field commanders, according to Sun Tzu,[5] must know how to lay plans and calculate, employ stratagems, position their assets, understand illusion versus reality, maneuver, and utilize intelligence (research) data. The bottom line is that Sun Tzu's theories have practical implications and applications in today's world of corporate competition. And you will have a greater chance of survival (and then success) if your Gyroscope is finely tuned and true to course.

A Bizarro Universe

In a compelling *New York Times* column, Disaster and Denial, Paul Krugman acknowledges:

> When I first began writing for The Times, I was naïve about many things, but my biggest misconception was this: I actually believed that influential people could be moved by evidence, that they would change their views if events completely refuted their beliefs.[6]

Krugman reminds us that regulator types

> …[live in] a bizarro universe in which government bureaucrats, not greedy bankers, caused the meltdown, … government-sponsored agencies triggered the crisis, … a universe in which regulators coerced banks into making loans to unqualified borrowers, even though only one of the top 25 subprime lenders was subject to the regulations in question.

---

[5]Please refer to page 85 of "War Is Hell, Business Ain't: Applying Sun Tzu's 'The Art of War'" for more on Sun Tzu.

[6]*The New York Times*, December 13, 2009.

Krugman astutely reminds us of a principle enunciated so eloquently by Upton Sinclair: "It's difficult to get a man to understand something when his salary depends on his not understanding it."

So, how does the FP survive and prosper in a potentially corrupt environment, one that, shall we say, is sometimes riddled with betrayal—betrayal demonstrated by poor upper-level corporate decision making and spending? Betrayal manifested by obscenely high bonuses based on lame products made to fail "down the road." (Genius-caliber hedge fund managers can capitalize on bubbles.)

A negative corporate culture plays on all of the FP's vulnerabilities, making him even more prone to codependency, a false sense of confidence and trust, loneliness, anxiety, and stress. Assuming the FP's decision is to remain within this environment, he must cultivate ways of becoming his own, insulated, self-protected entity, one that can balance its energies and expectations in service to himself, his company, and his clients.

The smart, happy, and successful FP must create his own Gyroscope in order to travel safely through the storm and chaos of corporate culture and the unpredictable volatility of the market that could crush weaker souls in nanoseconds.

The Right Tools, the Wrong Hands

Since the 1970s, the National Rifle Association has bandied about a clever slogan: "Guns don't kill people, people kill people." Depending on your viewpoint, this catchphrase is either woefully irresponsible or quite profound. British comedian Eddie Izzard clarified a key point when he said: "The National Rifle Association says that guns don't kill people, people do. *But I think the guns help.*"[7]

The Wall Psychologist's Gyroscope is intended to inspire you to consistently seek clarity across the murky landscape that is the financial services industry. Not everything is as it appears. Borrowing a way with words from our friends at the NRA, I advise my clients: "Hedge funds don't crush markets; irresponsible, narcissistic financial psychopaths crush

---

[7]E. Izzard. 1999. "Dressed to Kill," an HBO special.

markets." Just as a gun can be used to kill, a hedge fund can be manipulated by sinister forces to inflict great harm. Hedge funds are not inherently evil. Sure, from the outside looking in, it is difficult not to despise the outsize gains and oft-offensive displays of ridiculous wealth—after all, to be human is to be jealous—but the key to assembling your Gyroscope is objectivity and balance, i.e., appreciating all the uses of the money gun and how it can be used as a vehicle for prosperity or twisted into a weapon of malice.

Speaking of which, what is a hedge fund? By definition, a hedge fund is:

> An aggressively managed portfolio of investments that uses advanced investment strategies, such as leveraged, long, short and derivative positions in both domestic and international markets with the goal of generating high returns (either in an absolute sense or over a specified market benchmark). Legally, hedge funds are most often set up as private investment partnerships that are open to a limited number of investors and require a very large initial minimum investment. Investments in hedge funds are illiquid, as they often require that investors keep their money in the fund for at least 1 year. (Shortman 2010)

Alfred W. Jones, an Australian with a PhD in Sociology from Columbia University, created the first such fund in 1949. Hedge funds gained momentum in the 1970s and have been rapidly expanding in prominence and value ever since. Ironically, the term "hedging" reflects the practice of attempting to reduce risk, although the primary objective of most hedge funds is to maximize return on investment, which often runs counter to risk aversion. Additionally, as pools of accredited investors (each required to possess a net worth of more than $1 million, along with having to satisfy other criteria), hedge funds are not as heavily regulated as are mutual funds.

And what happens when either misguided or marginally responsible individuals arrive at this nexus of minimally regulated financial power?

Long-Term Capital Management (LTCM) happens.

Learning a Lesson the Hard Way

For the uninitiated, the stunning flameout of LTCM was the igniting spark that led to the market implosion of the late 1990s. Deregulation and bailout protocols developed during this period guided the government's approach during subsequent, more recent meltdowns.

A number of my clients have worked for hedge funds based in Stamford and Greenwich, Connecticut. The operational style of hedge funds headquartered in these two affluent redoubts established the tone and mentality for the market free-for-all that precipitated the Great Recession of 2009.

LTCM was a U.S. hedge fund that used trading strategies such as fixed-income arbitrage, statistical arbitrage, and pairs trading, combined with enormously high leverage. Founded in 1994 by John Meriwether, the former vice-chairman and head of bond trading at Salomon Brothers, LTCM had on its Board of Directors Myron Scholes and Robert C. Merton, who shared the 1997 Nobel Prize in Economics.

Initially meeting with enormous success, the hedge fund had annualized returns of more than 40 percent (after fees) in its early years, but in 1998 LTCM lost an estimated $4.6 billion in less than 4 months following the Russian financial crisis and folded in early 2000. Niall Ferguson points out that the LTCM partners forgot their history vis-à-vis the 1917 Russian default during their Russian Revolution. In his recent book, *The Ascent of Money: A Financial History of the World*, Ferguson cunningly refers to LTCM as "Short-Term Capital Mismanagement."

The principals at LTCM parlayed their financial star power, trading on their credentials, to lure clients into an endeavor that was going to make tons of money—until "genius failed" in 1999, and the New York Federal Reserve, in concert with 14 banks, bailed LTCM out so that the financial system would not collapse. Prior to the collapse of LTCM, the fund had years in which the partners charged a 2 percent management fee and received 25 percent of the annual profit. In some years, the gross profit was $8 billion, and so each partner "earned" an extra $250 million.

Acclaimed business writer Roger Lowenstein dubbed LTCM collectively 'a band of geniuses' in his best-selling book *When Genius Failed: The Rise and Fall of LTCM*, although some might be inclined to contend that genius is a body of work, not money made with volatile financial products ultimately destined to fail because of their creators' and handlers' lack of a true understanding and appreciation of risk theory.

Analysis of the Mind of a Magnificent Failure

Eric Rosenfeld had a PhD from MIT and arrived on Wall Street via the traditional route: Harvard Business School, landing at the prestigious firm of Salomon Brothers. Later, he left Salomon to join Meriwether at LTCM. Years later, when the smoke from the fiasco cleared, Rosenfeld assumed the role of champion of LTCM on the lecture circuit and, as such, he has been the focus of many business writers. I recall his lecture at the MIT Sloan School in February 2009, available as a webcast.

I remember that for several weeks, many of my clients shared fascinating personal observations with me regarding Rosenfeld's performance. They claimed that they had rarely seen in an individual such a concentration of arrogance, greed, money lust, mania, bluster, and world class rationalization/intellectualization mechanisms. The deeper I dug, the harder it was for me to dismiss their observations.

Rosenfeld engaged his audience by asking the group whether they had heard of LTCM and its downfall. When they answered yes, he responded: "It never ends," as if in some way he was victimized. "It never goes away," he reiterated, seemingly because the LTCM's spectacular burnout etched a template for future Wall Street failures that nearly took the entire financial system down, each in its own fell swoop. Rosenfeld asserted: "We had enormous risk that got out of control." He then accused his critics of having "an anti-intellectual tint with anything associated with LTCM." He discussed what he conceptualized as the top 10 myths and misconceptions about LTCM.

They started in 1994 with $1.1 billion in capitalization. LTCM had been, at its conception, the largest startup hedge fund to date. The partners put up $100 million of their own money. How did it all go so wrong? Rosenfeld described huge, hugely leveraged positions, some at up to 300:1. I found myself wondering how anyone could possibly justify such irresponsible exposure. The truly valuable question is: What was the value of what LTCM was doing? Was there even inherent value in their enterprise? Clearly, they were in the business to make money, but at what cost? Was the mission of this enterprise simply the pursuit of money for the sake of accumulating money? Has justification à la Rosenfeld so deeply seated itself in the financial mind that any and all means are justified if the end is accomplished?

Finally, at what point did LTCM's principals realize that they had squarely left behind any smidgen of vestige of the spirit of fiduciary responsibility?

Objective Self-Examination Is Essential to Success

The Wall Street Psychologist's Gyroscope encourages periodic self-examination that includes a refresh on key concepts, such as fiduciary responsibility. It also requires an intimate understanding of the concept and application of the practice of virtue. Once you have performed the requisite internal inventory and exercises, it becomes possible to avoid the pitfalls that dragged LTCM to its knees.

When they lack the desire or the ability to use such self-auditing mechanisms, highly intelligent people seek justifications elsewhere. Rosenfeld claimed Warren Buffet would have bought LTCM for $250 million, but they couldn't contact him as Buffet was out of town and not easy to reach on a new satellite-link phone.

In *When Genius Failed*, Roger Lowenstein confirms the fact that Buffet wanted to buy LTCM but qualifies the bare fact with a key addendum— after meeting with Rosenfeld and Meriwether, Buffet backed out of the deal. Goldman Sachs, AIG, and Berkshire Hathaway then offered to buy out the fund's partners for $250 million, to inject $3.75 billion into LTCM, and to operate it as part of Goldman's own trading division. On September 23, 1998, the offer was rejected. The same day, the Federal Reserve Bank of New York organized a bailout of $3.625 billion by the major creditors to avoid a wider collapse of the financial markets.

Many viewed the LTCM bailout as a bailout for the rich, a precursor to the "Too Big to Fail" concept, with which we are now all too familiar— shades of AIG, Bank of America, Citigroup, and Mammon knows who else in the future. Rosenfeld, however, continues to deflect responsibility.

He has actually implied that LTCM took on more and more risk because they knew the Federal Reserve would back them. Assuming this, every LTCM move was calculated, every angle considered, every hedge contemplated, and they became expert at manipulating their lenders and credit sources. And this is genius?

"It was only a couple of billion dollars, who cares?" "It happens," Rosenfeld says in the lecture. He then goes on about the prisoner's dilemma, a poignantly ironic reference, given the situation. He claims the solution for LTCM was to minimize their losses, but it all happened so fast, they sped down the slope too quickly. He then quips, "Bear Sterns got theirs," laughing over the graves of his competitors. But there is enough cynicism to go around—when discussing the fact that LTCM partners lost $2 billion, Rosenfeld laughs it off: "We Madoffed ourselves." He discusses endogenous risk and risk control, claiming that LTCM was built on diversification.

A fascinating feature and key takeaway of this lecture is the belief system as portrayed by the attitude of one of Wall Street's best and brightest: "We are right, even when we are wrong"; lack of perspective, lack of contrition, few to no scruples, relativistic/opportunistic morality. These attitudes persist today and are discussed in the section of this book that covers Alan Greenspan's "confession."

The operational style and character of LTCM foreshadowed the governing dynamics of the Wall Street mentality, which, in concert with Big Government, created the Great Recession of 2009.

Fast-Forward to Today

After the bailout, LTCM continued operations. Over the next year, it earned 10 percent. By early 2000, the fund had been liquidated, and the consortium of banks that financed the bailout had been paid back, but the collapse was devastating for many involved.

Goldman Sachs' CEO Jon Corzine, who had been closely involved with LTCM, was forced out in a boardroom coup led by Henry Paulson. David W. Mullins, once considered a possible successor to Alan Greenspan, saw his future with the Federal Reserve dashed. The theories of Merton and Scholes took a public beating. In its annual reports, Merrill Lynch observed that mathematical risk models "may provide a greater sense of security than warranted; therefore, reliance on these models should be limited."

After helping to unwind LTCM, Meriwether launched JWM Partners. Haghani, Hilibrand, Leahy, and Rosenfeld all signed up as principals of the new firm. By December 1999, they had raised $250 million for a fund that would continue with many of LTCM's strategies, this time using less leverage. Given the credit crisis, however, JWM Partners was hit with a 44 percent loss in its Relative Value Opportunity II fund from September 2007 through February 2009. The JWM Hedge Fund was shut down in July 2009.

These days Rosenfeld alerts audiences that "it makes sense to be transparent" and that trades should be paired to control risk. But when it counted, LTCM was not doing this, especially with regards to those lethal Russian bonds. Toward the end of the MIT lecture, Rosenfeld finally acknowledges: "Our risk management was wrong. You have to be able to manage in the bad days." He also puts in a dig at the banks and brokers, and their lack of professionalism: "You pay them to do due diligence and they end up with Madoff."

At the end, Rosenfeld tells a story about a "rocket scientist" kid from Cal Tech who can build wonderful mathematical models, but is not able to deliver new products. He compares this person to an "outlier," a new hire with imagination and intuition. He finishes his lecture by professing his interest these days: ".... less about math and more about intuition and curiosity." Before, he says, he would "get a signal" from a potential new hire, and act accordingly. It would seem that his experience at LTCM sharpened his focus and put him more in touch with criterion behavior— i.e., what an individual can bring to the table—and less likely to be distracted by someone's bare pedigree.

Still, does the convenience of a villain and incompetent regulators and auditors restore the damage wrought?

It is through self-reflection and an honest insistence on objectivity, due diligence, and integrity in decision making that a FP has a higher likelihood of avoiding the enduring shame of becoming a byword for fundamental financial failure.

The Banality of Corruption

In 1963, German–Jewish political theorist Hannah Arendt reported on the Adolph Eichmann trial in Jerusalem for *The New Yorker* magazine. Her reporting was eventually turned into a book, *Eichmann in Jerusalem: A Report on the Banality of Evil.*

Arendt's views caused a stir in 1963, especially within the context of the Holocaust, as she questioned whether evil is always a contrived maliciousness or perhaps a result of thoughtlessness. Certainly, the man known as "The Architect of the Holocaust" seemed to be the embodiment of pure evil.

In the context of financial malfeasance and destruction of the fiduciary responsibility between bank and buyer, broker and client, it makes sense to seek the answer to a question asked about those who destroy the responsibility to stay human and humane, those who murder on command. That question is: Can ordinary people be conditioned to blindly obey orders without applying the faculty of critical thinking? This is a very troubling issue for all of us.

The Ubiquity of Evil

Arendt's work is all the more compelling when one takes up her argument that many of the great evils throughout history have been perpetrated by ordinary people in extraordinary circumstances. Consider her controversial coinage: "the banality of evil." Those who did not live through those dark times might find it difficult to truly apprehend the context of its creation. That context is the Final Solution, the implementation of which exterminated millions of Jews, homosexuals, the mentally and physically ill, clergy, and countless others.

In employing the term *banal*, Arendt was neither minimizing nor excusing the severity of these atrocities. Rather, she was hypothesizing that these actions were not necessarily the product of supremely malicious or murderous intent, but more so instances of willful participation in organized violence, made possible by psychological conditioning that led to pathological lack of judgment and complete disregard for the humanity and value of others.

Eichmann was the architect of the Final Solution, but Arendt did not find him to be particularly diabolical. He was a masterful administrator who, like so many thousands of German officers and soldiers, was following orders. He was certainly responsible for his actions, and the responsibility for his actions extended well beyond what concerned him as an individual. Indeed, it was his efficiency and effectiveness as an organizer that propelled him to the position where he would ultimately design and oversee the wholesale extermination of so many human beings.

Yet it took psychological conditioning to remove morality from the equation. Although many in Nazi Germany, especially those in power, were certainly psychopathic, the overwhelming majority of soldiers and citizens in the Germany of the time were capable of empathy. It took the psychological conditioning of the majority by the propaganda machine to lead to the stripping away of its human element, its inherent sense of morality—at least as it applied to certain minorities. There are many accounts of German soldiers who were not ardent anti-Semites yet followed barbaric orders without question.

Arendt takes her theory further, to indicate that Eichmann was actually incapable of exercising the judgment that would have elicited empathy from him for the plight of his victims. What made him so effective, she says, was not his hatred of the Jews, but rather his lack of critical thinking and incapacity for genuine empathy, which is required for the humanization of victims. Eichmann would have had to employ self-reflection as a component of his judgment process, to envision the consequences of his actions.

Lacking the faculty of empathy and the capacity to employ it is a typical characteristic of psychopathic behavior. Was Eichmann psychopathic? Of course he was. Yet I think it is safe to say that the whole of the German people was not; and yet so many were directly complicit in such atrocities. What's the lesson here?

Wall Street Corruption Is Systemic

Nazi Germany is an extreme example, yet based on my practice experience and the well-chronicled events that have taken place on Wall Street over the last several years, I am certainly inclined to agree with Arendt's theories and, paraphrasing, to assert that modern-day Wall Street culture suffers from the banality of corruption.

For many on Wall Street, deception, lies, the manipulation of data, and self-interested behaviors are the order of the day, yet the people committing these acts are not all inherently evil. While many exhibit a seeming disregard for morality, along with a lack of empathy, they are not clinically psychopathic, nor did they begin to display these characteristics immediately on entering the industry. These traits are developed over long time spans, bolstered by being sanctioned, although not always explicitly, by the corporate regime. Corruption is commonplace on the Street, to the point of banality. FPs need to be aware of this systemic corruption; it is indigenous in their culture.

The baseline attitude base goes something like this:

> We will do our thing, push the edge of the envelope, and then see if we get caught. We know your resources are limited. We have the power, the money, and the capacity to hire the best lawyers to plead our case. In a war of attrition we will probably prevail. We are the true Masters of the Universe. We have entitlements and we strut the Earth righteously as we should. We are not humble, nor are we required to be.

These sentiments have actually been expressed, using these words, by many of my clients holding highly placed Wall Street corporate positions.

Wall Street CEOs are not easily recognized psychopaths. Their mission is to turn a profit any way they can. They can say one thing and do another. The means justify the ends in their world. Profits are the only thing that counts. However, if one compares Blankfein at Goldman and O'Neal at Merrill, one gets very interesting results. Bethany McLean and Joe Nocera document these differences in their new book, *All the Devils Are Here* (Mcclean and Nocera 2010). O'Neal did not solicit diverse opinions; Blankfein did, which largely served Goldman well and strengthened their capacity to survive and prosper. This type of behavior is common—seemingly universal—on the Street, and one does not have to look like a psychopathic killer or a gang member to be one while running a major financial corporation.

Few have it in them to sacrifice themselves, but you do not have to be a whistleblower to distance yourself from corruption. There are always consequences to complicity, and sooner or later they catch up with you.

The Milgram Obedience Experiments

How far would you go to obey authority?

At roughly the same time when Arendt was developing her thesis on the basis of the Eichmann trial, Yale University psychologist Stanley Milgram conducted a series of landmark experiments investigating obedience to authority. Milgram enlisted 40 men to participate in the experiment, which involved a machine generating electric shocks starting at 30 volts and increasing in 15-volt increments up to 450 volts. These levels were indicated on switches labeled "slight shock," "moderate shock," and "danger: severe shock." The last two switches were marked with a sinister "XXX."

Participants were each assigned the role of "teacher," requiring them to deliver a shock to the "student" every time an incorrect answer was provided. The participants had no reason to suspect they were not delivering painful shocks to the students, although the students were actually actors pretending to be shocked.

As the experiment wore on, the participants could hear the student plead for release or complain of heart conditions or other ailments. As the voltage exceeded the 300-volt level, the student/actor was instructed to bang on the wall and insist on release. At this point, the student/actor refused to answer the questions posed to them, and the participant/teacher was instructed to treat any lack of an answer as a wrong answer and administer a shock.

Most participants asked the experimenter whether they should continue. The experimenter issued a series of commands meant to prod the participant into continuing with the experiment:

- "Please continue."
- "The experiment requires that you continue."

- "It is absolutely essential that you continue."
- "You have no other choice; you must go on."

How far do you think most participants were willing to go? The results were quite disturbing.

When Milgram presented this question to a group of Yale University students, they responded that no more than 3 out of 100 participants would deliver the maximum shock. Actually, some 65 percent delivered maximum shocks. A stunning 26 of the 40 participants delivered maximum shocks, 14 stopping before they reached that level. Milgram also reported that many of the participants became angry, aggravated, and distraught. Still, they obeyed the orders, many of them all the way up to and including the maximum shock, by which they thought they were actually killing people.

Milgram summarized the experiment in a 1974 article, *The Perils of Obedience*, writing:

Ordinary people simply doing their jobs, and without any particular hostility on their part, can become agents in a terrible, destructive process. Moreover, even when the destructive effects of their work become patently clear and they are asked to carry out actions incompatible with fundamental standards of morality, relatively few people have the resources needed to resist authority.

As is my professional practice, The Wall Street Psychologist's Gyroscope is designed to revisit morality, reset the moral compass, and rethink key virtues to avoid the pitfalls of the banality of corruption and blind obedience.

Ignoring the Warning Signs

Hindsight vision may be 20/20, but does foresight in the financial services industry need to be nearly blind? Why do markets *crash* and bubbles *burst*? Why does epic disaster rush upon this industry so suddenly and terribly? The Wall Street Psychologist's Gyroscope is a vehicle designed to help you gain and maintain a grounded perspective in the money-mad world of financial services.

Ask Yourself Not How You Are Investing, But Why

Again, The Wall Street Psychologist's Gyroscope is not an investment philosophy. In treatment, I do not review my clients' portfolios with them. I do not look at what they invest in, but rather at what drives their decision-making processes and their emotional life. Ultimately, when you make the right decisions for the right reasons—or even the wrong decisions for the right reasons—you temper insecurity and build self-assuredness.

You enhance your professional relationships, both as client and as provider. Not only do you limit your exposure, but, should disaster strike, you minimize the guilt and self-loathing that could otherwise plunge you into another bout of depression or self-destructive behavior. To illustrate the point, consider the time line below that led up to the destruction of Lehman Brothers—the event that ushered in the most recent market debacle and subsequent recession.

February 27, 2007	Freddie Mac (Federal Home Loan Mortgage Corp.) announces that it will stop buying the most risky subprime mortgages/mortgage-related securities.
April 2, 2007	Major subprime lender New Century Financial Corp. files for Chapter 11 bankruptcy protection.
June 1, 2007	More than 100 bonds backed by second-lien subprime mortgages downgraded by Standard and Poor's and Moody's Investor Services.
June 7, 2007	Bear Stearns alerts investors that it is suspending redemptions from its High-Grade Structured Credit Strategies Enhanced Leverage Fund.
July 11, 2007	612 securities backed by subprime residential mortgages placed on a credit watch by Standard and Poor's.
July 24, 2007	Countrywide Financial Corp. issues guidance of "difficult conditions."

July 31, 2007	Bear Stearns liquidates two hedge funds that specialize in mortgage-backed securities.
August 6, 2007	American Home Mortgage Investment Corp. seeks Chapter 11 bankruptcy protection.
January 1, 2008	On the verge of collapse, mortgage lender Countrywide Financial is bought out by Bank of America, at a substantial discount.
March 24, 2008	Facing collapse, investment bank Bear Sterns is purchased by JPMorgan Chase.
July 11, 2008	The Office of Thrift Supervision shutters IndyMac Bank, handing deposits over to the Federal Deposit Insurance Corporation (FDIC) for protection.
July 15, 2008	To protect mortgage lenders, the Securities and Exchange Commission (SEC) temporarily prohibits the naked short selling of the securities of Fannie Mae, Freddie Mac, and primary dealers at commercial and investment banks.
September 7, 2008	On the brink of collapse, Fannie Mae and Freddie Mac are placed into government conservatorship.
September 15, 2008	Plagued by toxic assets, Merrill Lynch is forced to sell itself to Bank of America.
September 15, 2008	As Lehman Brothers fails, the Dow Jones Industrial Average plummets more than 500 points in a single day.

Plenty of warning signs went unheeded. Next time—when there is a next time—will you see the train coming? Even on the brink of disaster with all the writing on the wall, the human psyche clings to hope, revels in denial, and just won't wake up and smell the coffee! The power of the status quo and faith in our institutions—however gossamer and largely dependent on our belief in them in order to persist—are simply too powerful for most of us. Fear of change, fear of the unknown, and a lack of appreciation of the surreal color our perceptions all the time.

Would You Prefer Not to?

In 1853 famed American novelist Herman Melville published *Bartleby, the Scrivener: A Story of Wall Street*, a novella. It is the story of Bartleby, the third scrivener hired by a wealthy Manhattan lawyer (and the narrator) to copy legal documents and run his office efficiently. From the outset Bartleby appears to be an asset to the practice, but one day he snaps and when asked by his employer to proofread a copied document, Bartleby responds, "I'd prefer not to." This soon becomes Bartleby's stock response to all requests.

His productivity plummets, while he actually moves into the office, as he appears to have no life outside of work. Bartleby becomes the consummate control freak, with a healthy dose of a not-so-latent passive-aggressive personality disorder thrown in for flavor. His employer ends up relocating his practice to escape Bartleby. The new tenant has Bartleby forcibly evicted, and Bartleby winds up in the infamous Tombs jail, where he ultimately starves himself to death, having preferred not to eat.

Over the years there have been many interpretations of the various themes that course through this work. It is surely a well-scripted account of a descent into depression and madness. It is also a powerful example of how one person's mental illness can paralyze that person as well as many around him—in this case, an entire business operation.

I do not pretend to have access to the inner sanctums of Wall Street, nor can I peer into the minds of its masterminds. When it comes to the Wall Street debacle du jour, the media invariably distorts the facts, while jailhouse interviews provide conflicting testimony as to what really happened. I am not so quick to condemn these architects of disaster. However, I think that in the furthest recesses of their minds many of these tycoons must have found themselves in so deep a tailspin that when the worm turned, it must have brought out in them a bit of Bartleby.

Whether it is Enron or Tyco or Lehman or any number of the smaller implosions that have littered the Street in recent years, when they perform the autopsy of the disaster, they invariably identify key turning points at which inaction set the company on the path to a fiasco. Yet it is about more than just the chief executive. In most instances, there is complicity all the way down the line. Deep inside, they're just ignoring the warning signs in a desperate hope things may turn around or disaster may be avoided or someone else may swoop in and save the day. It can never happen to us.

All too often, when it comes to self-assessing and facing the hard realities, we are too quick to prefer not to. Psychologically, we have an affinity for the positive. It is human instinct to turn away from bad news.

In the third section of the book, where we explore the components of the Wall Street's Psychologist's Gyroscope, there is a section, entitled *Developing a Personal Risk Management Strategy*, within which I provide a basic questionnaire. It asks you to invest the time and ask yourself the hard questions that, among other things, ensure that your personal investment philosophy is sound and that you are not especially likely to succumb to the weak points of your psyche. Ultimately, this is one more component of The Wall Street Psychologist's Gyroscope, the maintenance of which will lead you down the path of psychological well-being and emotional security.

The Fatal Flaw Theory

The Fatal Flaw Theory is a key element of The Wall Street Psychologist's Gyroscope. The theory itself is nothing new. It posits that "if something seems too good to be true, it is too good to be true." In my practice, I urge my clients to embrace this simple maxim and incorporate it into their due diligence.

There are few sure things in the financial services arena; unfortunately, that short list includes the historical persistence of financial psychopaths who wreak havoc on the unsuspecting, gullible masses. No matter how many times something had proven to be too good to be true, there are always more than enough investors willing to overlook the obvious unlikelihood and unreality of something they are assured of as being solid and true and to plunge headlong into ill-advised schemes that almost always end in tears.

Our Susceptibility to Psychopaths

After 30 years of watching people willing to throw it all away because of a manic mélange of wishful thinking and pipe dreams cooked up and fed to them by master manipulators, I am no longer surprised to see even the most astute professionals fall prey to psychopathic predators. Why, you ask, are financial criminals able to perpetrate such outrageous, unconscionable frauds? The answer is inextricable from our psychological relationship with money and the fact that we are all genetically predisposed to aspirations of survival and dominance.

Deep down, we all feel entitled. We all believe that someday our ship will come in; the brass ring will present itself; the crowds part; confetti shower down; the sailor will kiss the girl; and the 15 minutes or longer of fame, recognition, and reward that are rightfully ours will be presented to us on a sterling silver dish by a liveried butler in white kid gloves. It is, you see, textbook human nature to look askance at reason and likelihood, to elevate the most desperate of hopes into the realm of the spoken-for future. In other words, we have an inborn bias for seeing the aspired for as the actual and for doubling down on the thing we desire, in spite of doubt and better judgment.

Never were these dangerous human traits exploited more effectively than in the course of the unfortunate saga of Bernard "Bernie" Madoff, responsible for the largest financial crime ever perpetrated by a single person. His was a fantastic criminal enterprise going back to the 1980s and involving a staggering $65 billion.[8] On June 29, 2009, Madoff was sentenced to 150 years in prison. Still, the verdict rang hollow, given the thousands (14,000-plus) of people whose finances were crippled by Madoff's actions. That many of the victims should have known better is entirely beside my point.

I developed The Wall Street Psychologist's Gyroscope as a treatment technique, a regimen for self-empowerment and self-improvement, which, among other things, requires the practitioner to erect psychological defenses so as to minimize susceptibility to financial malfeasance.

The Madoff scandal, though remarkable in scope, is not unique. Although his particular version of it was quite complex, what Madoff had been bringing off for years was a variation of the Ponzi scheme, a fraudulent investment enterprise in which the perpetrator pays returns

---

[8] The court-appointed trustee estimated actual losses to investors, when paper and promised returns were removed from the equation, to be $18 billion.

to investors from their own money or money paid in by subsequent investors. There are few or no actual profits generated by the enterprise. As proven by Madoff's success, the scheme is so attractive because the investor is offered returns whose size and consistency his money manager's competitors simply cannot match.

The scheme is uncovered sooner or later by regulators or collapses under the weight of its ballooning financial obligations. In Madoff's case, because of his credibility, it took the market constriction of late 2008, when investors began withdrawing money en masse, for the scheme to unravel.

Falling for the Same Ruse Over and Over Again

The Ponzi scheme is named for Italian immigrant Charles Ponzi, who gained notoriety in the 1920s by enticing unsuspecting investors with the promise of amazing returns in the arbitrage of international reply coupons for postage stamps. Ponzi's pledge was that he could return a 50 percent profit within 45 days (or a 100 percent profit within 90 days) just by exchanging international postal reply coupons. In actuality, he quickly started to siphon money received from the more recent investors to pay the early ones, and kept the scam going as long as he could, taking in 40,000 people for a then-stunning $15 million.

First and foremost, The Wall Street Psychologist's Gyroscope espouses vigilance. Why? Because we all possess the belief that we are special and destined to have fantastic things happen to us. We do not want to be denied the finer things in life, and we all feel entitled to them. Like Ponzi, before him, what Madoff represented to the thousands of people he took in was the vehicle to power via prosperity.

Madoff's brilliance was in his having pushed the envelope far enough that the returns offered were substantial, but not so much that they were squarely beyond the realm of possibility. He was also consistent, regardless of market conditions, and, as former chairman of the NASDAQ (National Association of Securities Dealers Automated Quotations System), he underpinned his fraud with impeccable credentials, lulling his victims into a false sense of security.

Describing away the Madoff phenomenon as another example of human herd mentality barely scratches the surface of the real mechanisms at work. Ponzi schemes are simple yet dynamic because they exploit so many different facets of the relationship between the mind and money.

Madoff exploited every possible advantage, from his religious affiliation to the access he was afforded to elite social relationships, which he could plumb for credibility and further investment. At every turn, he offered the prospective investor entry into an exclusive realm of steady, high returns, which could facilitate a secure, affluent lifestyle, free of the instability and seeking that characterize the lives of mere mortals who are less rich or don't know Bernie Madoff. He told them what they wanted to hear. And they loved it.

Eliminating Vulnerability to Manipulation

My recommendation is to make a list of everything in your life to which the Fatal Flaw Theory may even remotely apply, where your return on your financial or emotional investment far exceeds expectations. This is an exercise in realism, not pessimism. As you review this list, ask yourself whether you have really done your due diligence. This will make for revelations, force you to make some honest admissions, and will most likely make you redouble your efforts at vigilance. It will also serve to condition you to act more responsibly toward yourself.

CHAPTER 2

Virtue, Balance, Tao, Gyroscope

The Wall Street Psychologist's Gyroscope is not a code of ethics, nor is it a moral road map. I am not here to preach a gospel, nor will I proselytize as an apostle of another's beliefs. You see, deep inside your mind, you already know your true path to enlightenment and wellness. And so, The Wall Street Psychologist's Gyroscope is merely a conduit that can be powered only by the self: self-awareness, self-discipline, self-control. After over 30 years of treating professionals in the financial services industry, if there is one thing I know, it is that repression of virtue is at the root of many psychological and physiological ailments. Of course, there are many other contributing factors to people's ills. As treatment progresses, we pull back the layers of years of moral capitulation, and my clients come to the sober realization that they have to answer for their actions. They must be accountable to themselves.

Understanding Virtue

What does it mean to be virtuous? From the Latin *virtus* and the Greek ἀρετη, virtue is the essence of moral excellence, manifested in all of its forms. Think of virtue as a quality or characteristic that is valued. Charity, creativity, compassion, justice, and wisdom are just some of the virtues one could mention (see the following list of all the virtues). To be virtuous is to seek excellence in yourself, in everything you do. It is quite telling that, in terms of definitions, the opposite of virtue is vice.

Examples of Virtues			
Acceptance	Generosity	Love	Sensitivity
Bravery	Gentleness	Loyalty	Simplicity
Caution	Gratitude	Majesty	Sincerity
Curiosity	Honesty	Moderation	Sobriety
Defiance	Humbleness	Obedience	Spontaneity
Determination	Humor	Openness	Steadfastness
Devotion	Impartiality	Patience	Strength
Discretion	Industry	Peace	Toughness
Flexibility	Innocence	Prudence	Tranquility
Focus	Justice	Reliability	Trust
Forgiveness	Kindness	Responsibility	Trustworthiness

Of course, you want and expect your financial professional (FP) to be focused, flexible, honest, just, loyal, client, prudent, responsible, sincere, steadfast, and trustworthy. In turn, these are essential ingredients of your own gyroscope. One client lives by the following adage, directed at his clients: "You have to trust me as much as I trust you." The components of virtue can only bolster the FP's emotional and professional life and ultimately make him better at what he does.

Virtue: Integrity

Integrity is another oft-misunderstood concept. Integrity comes from the Greek words *integritas* and *integra*, which mean "whole." In essence, integrity encompasses this sense of wholeness gained through consistency of character. An individual who has integrity is one who consistently strives to be faithful in action to his principles, often in the face of significant adversity.

An individual may have a core belief system, but might lack the strength of character, the integrity, to consistently act according to his principles. In some instances, acting contrary to the core principles the individual espouses is akin to hypocrisy, even cowardice. Anyone can be virtuous when it is convenient. It is displaying virtue in the face of physical or emotional harm, or under threat of financial loss, that shows integrity. Ultimately, whom would you trust in a dangerous situation—a competitor who is consistently truthful or a colleague who is frequently dishonest? This dilemma points to the essence of integrity.

Virtue: Dignity

The ancient Greeks, to whom modern Western society traces its social ideals, were well aware of basic human rights. Inspired by their ideas, Enlightenment-era thinkers saw human dignity as an incarnation of the idea that all human beings have an inalienable right to respect and ethical treatment. Indeed, dignity is closely associated with the right to virtue and autonomy.

It was also the Greeks that gave us the concept of hubris (or at least the word for it, from ancient Greek ὕβρις), referring to actions that humiliated the victim for the pleasure or gratification of the abuser. Hubris, seen as an exaggerated arrogance approaching narcissism, is common in the financial services industry. At its root, empathy despises and invalidates empathy, tolerance, and respect. Via subtle and direct action, often passive-aggressive behavior, hubris strips away dignity.

And yet, in a measure of poetic justice, the hubristic protagonist, oft-blinded by arrogance, hastens his own downfall. There are all too many examples of this phenomenon on modern-day Wall Street: Ken Lay, Richard Fuld, Bernard Madoff, Marc Dreier, and E. Stan O'Neal spring immediately to mind. Dignity is the preservation of the self through the appreciation of the rights of others. This is a critical concept for the FP, especially one who has gone astray, led by the Pied Piper of hubris. Interestingly, rehabilitation literally means the restoration of dignity. The gyroscope methodology described in this book shows how to achieve precisely that: to create, restore, and maintain dignity.

Virtue: Honor

Honor (derived from the Latin *honoris*) is the appraisal of a person's moral character on the basis of words and deeds. Honor may be seen as the sum of one's virtues and integrity. In many cultures, honor is integral to social stratification, and individuals are assigned a certain station based, in part, on adherence to an honor code. In relationships among men, honor is more often a justifying component of power, while with women honor has more to do with chastity and fidelity.

In the financial services industry, contractual obligations and regulations long ago supplanted widespread adherence to codes of honor. To act honorably, in the spirit of fairness, may place the individual at the mercy of those who would exploit every loophole and questionable tactic for an advantage. Still, honorable actions are extensions of virtuous behavior, and when applied with integrity (consistency), do much to enhance the reputation of the individual, thereby increasing the value of relational assets.

Looking at Life through Virtuous Eyes

Albert Einstein once said: "We can't solve problems by using the same kind of thinking we used when we created them." In order to build that personal gyroscope, the lost individual needs to change his mindset and tear down the repressive obstacles impeding growth. The person who honestly accepts accountability also enjoys the psychological salves of virtue, integrity, dignity, and honor. In the deepest recesses of the mind, no one is above personal reproach. No matter how we act, we know better. And only through internal honesty—honesty with ourselves—are we able to navigate morally ambiguous situations. When one is no longer repressing inner virtue, one is better able to develop a moral compass.

There is an adage that says that the man who can anger you can control you. When you aspire to virtue, integrity, dignity, and honor, you reinforce your sense of self and are, as a positive by-product, not so easily angered or manipulated. That does not come from a book or a lecture series or a website.

- It comes from within.
- It comes from building your gyroscope!

The Necessity of Balance, the Power of Tao

This book provides the FP with a variety of devices and tactics designed to help achieve personal *and* professional wellness—the two are inextricably intertwined. You see, thriving in this industry requires a level of commitment that consumes your life. There is no leaving the office at the office. Those I treat more often than not have severe problems achieving work–life balance. Although they may be successful in their climb up the corporate ladder and asset accumulation, they are frequently falling deeper and deeper into trouble in their personal relationships. Yet one can never quite reach an adequate level of fulfillment unless *both* sides of the coin are addressed.

For instance, I had one client who led a Wall Street firm, charged with oversight of the entire organization. He was revered, feared, and generously rewarded. In his mid-50s, he was a bright, handsome, and had distinctive angelic qualities.

His beginnings were humble. He came to the big city and hit the jackpot, both on Wall Street and when he found the love of his life. But this was not to be a fairy tale. There was no "happily ever after," at least not yet. Our hero plunged into the swirling cauldron that is Wall Street without first achieving inner balance. His modest background inspired an obsession with wealth accumulation and social climbing.

He surrendered his spirituality by yielding his virtue. His wife was a classic narcissistic, obsessed with herself and her beauty. She was, literally, trapped in the mirror. He developed an obsession with pornography and a lack of affection and intimacy bred insecurities, and suspicions abounded in his relationship until they separated—she began outwardly dating a retired police officer, and he started hooking up with 23-year old high school teacher that he had been chatting with for 2 years.

In light of the, apparent, mutual infidelity, my client was in a state of perpetual panic, because he knew that life as he knew it wouldn't last long. His lifestyle would invariably plummet, and he believed that his wife would double down on her previous threats and hire a ruthless divorce lawyer that would skewer him. His mission in therapy was to take stock of himself, face his sins, and attempt to lead a life guided by virtue and honor. Ultimately, in order to regain any semblance of wellness, he needed to achieve a virtuous balance in both his personal *and* professional lives.

The Essence of Balance

The value of this book is not in the specificity of its recommendations. Rather, it lies in providing a framework that enables the FP to envision his own path to self-fulfillment. That is why I encourage my readers to expand their thinking and explore different teachings and programs. If certain components of The Wall Street Psychologist's Gyroscope are not working for you, try others or try something else. Continue your quest. Find your path and hew to it.

The ancient Greeks contended that "the way people felt in their minds could influence the way they responded in their bodies" and vice versa. We can also compare this Western tenet with Eastern techniques that focus on meditation and the development of the meaning of one's life. One such ancient Eastern philosophy that I have found to be impressively effective in focusing my clients on the path to balance is the Tao, which, incidentally, means the way, or the path.

Taoism (or Daoism) refers to a range of religious and philosophical traditions that have influenced Eastern Asia for more than two millennia. Since roughly the early 19th century, Taoism had exercised an increasingly potent influence on the Western world. What is Taoism, in a sentence? It is an active, holistic concept of the world that emphasizes intuition over rationality,[1] observation over action.

Taoists also believe that change and transformation are the core aspects of life. They believe the natural world displays the dynamic interplay between the polar opposites of yin and yang. Opposites are linked in Taoism, and as such they formulate their own distinct kind of unity. Everything has a flip side, but that flip side is an inherent part of the whole. For example, the market goes up, then it has to go down; that's the market. There can be no market without cycles.

The Tao is the flow of the universe, the forces behind nature; and people are part of nature. Taoists talk of "effortless doing" and "less is

---

[1]Malcolm Gladwell's bestseller *Blink* speaks to a similar idea, contending that the human brain knows whether someone new is a friend or a foe in under two seconds, perhaps faster; in other words, you don't have to think about it, you just sense it.

more." The three Treasures of the Tao are moderation (simplicity), humility (modesty), and love (compassion).[2] The Tao is not static, nor should the FP be static, especially in stormy market conditions. Really—isn't the market ever stormy? This is why the FP must be willing to explore and embrace new philosophies—new ways of looking at the world, his job, his firm, his clients, himself.

Part of learning more about ourselves is considering the global context, the universe beyond. Knowing ourselves involves knowing how small and unimportant, and ultimately insignificant, we are; mere specks in the universe. Others have been here before us, and others will be here long after us. People gain peace and stability when they remind themselves that they are part of a long history of humanity; of a tradition of brothers and sisters; of people who have experienced the very same frustrations, pain, hardship, challenges, and struggles we are all enduring now.

I have treated some FPs who had experimented with and embraced the Tao, or another philosophy, and who claimed to be more at peace, more content as a result. Another thing—their production soared! They had achieved balance and, at the same time, sharpened their focus. The Tao teaches to yield so as not to break. Bent, you can straighten. Emptied, you can hold. Torn, you can mend. Philosophies like these are good approaches for any Wall Street denizen to adopt, for they help create a more consistent balance between one's work and inner life. After all, balance *is* everything.

Healing and Preventive Measures for the Mind–Body Connection

Any professional active in financial services should find something within the following pages that will be synonymous with their feelings and needs. My intention is not only to enable my readers and clients to address significant issues that have arisen in their lives and in the office, but also to

---

[2]The Three Treasures or Three Jewels first appear in Tao Te Ching, Chapter 67. The Tao Te Ching, most commonly attributed to Lao Tzu, is a classic Chinese text.

better equip them to avoid crises and calamities down the road. In previous sections, we established, on the basis of research and observation, the critical mind–body link—a highly complex relationship we are only now beginning to comprehend with any depth. Let us focus on that link and the ways in which it influences you.

Although researchers are ever making meaningful breakthroughs that are helping us to better define this connection, we can never fully know the extent of the consequences of risky behavior on either side of the mind–body relationship. In my career, spanning over 30 years, as a psychologist treating Wall Street professionals, I have witnessed the devastating ramifications of this link. Because of the nature of a FP's job description, and the associated lifestyle, psychological stressors have multiple definite, adverse physiological effects.

Moreover, many of my clients, consumed by greed and obsessed with power, have often disregarded common sense and caution, engaging in high-risk behavior with consequences for their health. Many who were not active substance abusers still did not lead healthy lifestyles, unless life events (hypertension, heart attack, obsessive compulsive disorder (OCD) behaviors, spousal ultimatums, severe debt, and overspending) conspired to make them face their pain and anguish.

The purpose of this section is to provide guidance for living a more health-conscious life. My recommendations are intended to be practical, as advice that is not reasonable and does not take into account the day-to-day pressures is not very good advice at all. This guidance includes various stress-mastery techniques, as well as active and passive relaxation techniques, visualization and imaging techniques, as well as compartmentalization techniques. I also don't just tell you to get more sleep, but give you advice on coping with sleep deprivation. Taking care of your mind and your body properly is as important as addressing any immediate psychological issues, as well as an absolutely crucial part of developing and maintaining a sound gyroscope.

The Components of the Gyroscope

Volume IV in this series presents a comprehensive description of the gyroscope. The gyroscope is a 360-degree self-creation/motivation model within which an individual selects from a wide range of proven best practices designed to provide incremental improvements in psychological and physical health. These enable the individual to better cope with the deception, betrayal, deep disappointment, severe financial loss, and the fear, loneliness, vulnerability, and panic that working on the Street can bring about. The sources of these phenomena and feelings are often rooted in interaction with clients or the corporate structure and can be beyond one's control. Still, how one copes with adversity is certainly within one's grasp.

Based on my years of experience, I felt compelled to write this book and to share the gyroscope methodology I created in order to improve and enrich the life of anyone who has to deal with money, as a professional or as an amateur.

Why gyroscope? A gyroscope is an apparatus with a central spinning wheel and a device called a gimbal, which allows the wheel's axle to maintain its orientation and equilibrium regardless of what is happening around it. An internal gyroscope allows anyone to hold steady in times of chaos and flux, and to maintain stability and thus survive and prosper, even when negotiating daily stresses, whether money related or not. If you are in touch with your inner and outer gimbals—your value system, work ethic, sense of well-being, duty, skill sets, relationships, and happiness parameters—you stand a much better chance of staying your desired course.

Reflect on the technical definition and characteristics of a gyroscope prescribed previously and note that an internal gyroscope allows the FP to hold steady in times of chaos and flux, to maintain stability and thus survive and prosper, even when negotiating the daily cycles of the market. Simply put, the gyroscope is a metaphorical methodology anyone can use to envision, storyboard, and achieve true, lasting personal and professional satisfaction.

The gyroscope is also a complete self-creation/motivation model offering a broad range of proven best practices designed to cause incremental improvements in psychological and physical health. I have found that the gyroscope is most needed by those working in high-stress professions, such as finance, which we are using as an illustrative model of society to understand the relationship between the mind and money.

So, how do you create and cultivate your gyroscope? That is the major focus of this book, namely, to outline the specific ways in which you can

(1) regain stability, (2) maintain equilibrium, and (3) empower yourself along the path of incremental improvement. The goals are better performance, realization of financial goals, and a healthy life–work balance. In this book, I teach you how to maintain the emotional equilibrium you need to attain and maintain.

As my clients work hard on developing their skill sets and inner life, the process becomes more sophisticated, engrossing, and productive. They develop from the inside out as people, and from the outside in as technically savvy FPs. They solve their problems in the field (office) and, ideally, become more fulfilled human beings internally—at home, at work, and everywhere in between. As we progress, they understand just how sacred fiduciary responsibility is, and how they must not create moral hazards so as not to ultimately suffer and subject the clients who trust them to suffering.

Creating one's own gyroscope is an intellectual, emotional, and spiritual process that permeates all aspects of one's life. Throughout the process we must keep in mind that people possess an emotional (limbic system) brain, and an analytic (frontoparietal cortex) brain. We are passionate, feeling human beings, yet we must bring to bear analytical skills and disciplined thinking in order to truly prosper in work and in life. How to harmonize these contrasting yet necessary brain systems is what I intend to share with you in this book.

In the pages that follow, we will meet people elevated by money's sway and swayed by its power to corrupt and eviscerate the soul; we will witness a cavalcade of sane, decent folks turned into compulsive addicts, hard-working strivers choked by getting what they wished for, ultra-entitled yuppies losing all touch with reality, floating off into dysfunctional sociopathy. We will also have a chance to cheer for them from our courtside seats, as they struggle back to reality, normality, psychological health, and truly successful lives—with my help and with the aid of the gyroscope methodology I've developed over decades of working with hundreds of clients, their inner balance disturbed by money's force field, their minds discombobulated by its propensity to put values, beliefs, and relationships to the test.

Money can leaven or leaden a life, make or break a worldview, build someone up, or hold them up on the way to balance and contentment.

I have seen the worst it can do to people, and I am here—not just to tell the scary tale, with tips on how to avoid it, but—to show you how to see money as an ingredient in your balance, instrument of your success, enabler of your victories.

There is a Latin motto, *Avia pervia*, which, loosely translated, means: "To make easy what is difficult to achieve." This is the essence of The Wall Street Psychologist's Gyroscope. It is a vehicle for self-awareness and self-improvement across the FP's physical, professional, and psychological dimensions. A gyroscope is fundamentally a device for maintaining and/or measuring orientation, and so we may apply the construct of a gyroscope as a metaphorical model for pursuing self-improvement and, in many instances, self-preservation.

The FP is immersed in the complex, ultra-competitive, constantly evolving landscape that is Wall Street. Whatever else they are, FPs are not passive individuals. My experience in treating them is that FPs can derive optimal benefit more easily by actively participating in their own remediation. To make this possible, I developed a series of internal and external processes for maintaining and measuring orientation. This is not a rigid step-by-step methodology. Complex regimens rarely produce meaningful, lasting results. Instead, I offer a collection of proven emotional/intellectual/physical/spiritual processes the FP can select from to integrate into his or her core with time and practice.

Start Simple to Build Momentum

My approach to treatment has its roots in the Orthogenic Principle, espoused by Heinz Werner (1890 to 1964), a noted Austrian developmental psychologist. According to Werner's principle, "Development proceeds from a state of relative lack of differentiation to a state of increasing differentiation and hierarchic integration"[3] in all aspects of an individual's life, from development to the management of life experience. Werner's principle can inspire hope because it reinforces the notion that, if one perseveres, one can grow, resolve conflict, and establish better operational

---

[3]H. Werne. 1952. *Comparative Psychology of Mental Development* (New York, NY: International Universities Press, Inc.).

methods in personal life and in business. In short, in treatment—as at work—we do not bite off more than we can psychologically chew. With proper guidance and development, getting this right gets easier to internalize and practice.

As my clients work hard on developing their skill sets and inner life, the process becomes more sophisticated, interesting, and sound. They develop *from the inside out* as persons, and *from the outside in* as technically savvy FPs. Problems are solved in the field (office), and, ideally, they become more fulfilled human beings internally (at home, at work, and everywhere in between). As we progress, they understand just how sacred fiduciary responsibility is and how they must not create moral hazards so as not to ultimately suffer and subject the clients who have trusted them to suffering.

Creating one's own gyroscope is an intellectual, emotional, and spiritual process that permeates one's professional and personal lives. However, we must keep in mind that people possess an emotional (limbic system) brain and an analytic (frontoparietal cortex) brain. Harmonizing these contrasting but necessary brain systems is my mission in this book. We are passionate, feeling human beings, but we must exercise disciplined, analytical skills and thinking in order to truly prosper on the Street. These contrasting skills/forces/states of being challenge FPs daily, especially from 9:30am to 4pm Eastern Standard Time.

FPs form a class of client unlike any other. Owing to the nature of their jobs, they are driven by the tangible. They need a project plan, a series of metrics, something concrete to help them envision a path to recovery. That's where the gyroscope comes in. The journey will be hard, but starting out on it need not be too much so; having an action matrix provides a detailed, measured plan of improvement that reinforces the what of the end goal with the how of the process.

Simply put, the gyroscope is a metaphorical methodology using which the individual can storyboard a strategy to achieving true, lasting personal and professional satisfaction. Think of the tactics and techniques on the following pages as elements of your project plan to execute, based on the research previously provided in this book.

Specifically, the first section of this book raises awareness about the cause of many psychological maladies afflicting FPs. I then lead my readers through the effect, as in the psychological and physiological consequences of the inherent stress of their jobs, and the impact of negative behavior and poor choices. Along that trajectory, we now arrive at The Wall Street Psychologist's Gyroscope, to provide the guidance necessary to address the various issues we explored previously. Remember, treatment of the body and the mind constitutes the sum of many parts.

An À la Carte Approach to Treatment

To get started, the individual needs to select one or more components of The Wall Street Psychologist's Gyroscope that are easily attainable. As they achieve success, they select additional components, and the process of self-improvement becomes more sophisticated. Problems are solved, incremental gains are made, and progress soon becomes a constant theme in the FP's life. Like every individual I treat, every gyroscope we build is unique, yet there is commonality of both condition and treatment. With these tools, you can develop your own gyroscope that will allow you to dig deeper, explore your true identity, and mine your psyche as a means of identifying ways to improve and maintain orientation. Based on that premise, a visualization of the gyroscope is provided here. All of these elements are individually explained in Volume IV, which includes comprehensive descriptions of each technique, and a model of a gyroscope superimposed with labels that define the functionality of the methodology relative to the techniques presented.

Gyroscope Methodology
Techniques and Strategies for Creating Balance*

- Client Categorization Strategy
- Communications Best Practices
- Compartmentalization Strategy
- Personal Exit Strategy
- Expectation Management Strategy
- Personal Risk Management Strategy
- Personal Wellness Strategy
- Relationship Management Strategy— An "Equilibrium-Based" Approach
- Reputation Protection Strategy
- Work-Environment Survival Strategies
- Exercises & Best Practices
- Breathing Exercises
- Fiduciary Responsibility Affirmation
- Getting Your Yoga on
- Guilt Management Techniques

- Legal Liability Protection Action Plan
- Meditation Techniques
- Panic, Impulsivity, and Impatience Methodology
- Personal "Rules of Engagement"
- Personal Deception Avoidance Techniques
- Personal Mission Statement
- Personal Return on Investment (ROI) Calculator
- Progressive Muscle Relaxation Techniques
- Realistic Diet & Exercise Regimen
- Signaling Theory Best Practices
- Sleep Deprivation Coping Techniques
- Substance Abuse Rehabilitation Options
- Success Benchmarking
- Support Network Plan
- Visual Imaging Techniques

* Book 4 provides comprehensive descriptions of each technique and a gyroscope diagram superimposed with labels that define the functionality of the methodology relative to the techniques presented.

What the Gyroscope Is Not

Let me make an important distinction. The Wall Street Psychologist's Gyroscope is not an investment philosophy. I am not an investment advisor, nor am I some financial guru. I do not even preach caution in investment practices for the sole sake of being conservative. Risk is good, when engaged in for the right reasons. Risk based on a balanced and correct interpretation of market fundamentals can make you successful. Risk driven by insecurity and a willingness to succumb to herd mentality, to catch the latest wave, can destroy entire markets, even lay waste to global economies.

I am both student and teacher of the behavioral patterns of FPs. The simple fact is that crises do not happen all of a sudden. They build over the course of time, slowly gathering momentum until they crash in violent cascades that ripple across the globe, upending the security of billions of people with their tumult and wake. The warning signs were always there. They always are. As I say to my clients, you do not need 20/20 hindsight to instill in yourself the discipline that will remove the psychological blinders that stifle preventive measures.

Additionally, as with suggestions in any other self-help book, the reader should note that the advice offered in my books should not be considered substitutes for professional psychological treatment and therapy. The self-help contents are solely the opinion of the author and should not be considered as a form of therapy, advice, direction, and/or diagnosis or treatment of any kind: medical, spiritual, mental, or other. Instead, the advice included is designed to serve as a component of an improvement process, augmenting whatever treatment may be taking place by trained professionals. If expert advice or counseling is needed, the services of a competent professional should be sought.

CHAPTER 3

Money, Mind, Morality

What is your interpretation of morality? What is the essence of dignity?

Moral Bankruptcy Proceedings

I recall one case, in particular, in which I worked with a consultant who managed millions and billions of dollars in assets. He was very good at what he did. However, he had a weakness for young women and alcohol. When he entered treatment, he was morally bankrupt, and his production was tanking. At some point, his perspective grew dark. Life became a constant grind, yet he could not understand the source of his increasing depression and anxiety.

My client confessed that he no longer felt whole, or even remotely happy. As we explored his emotions, he revealed that his dignity was eroding and his honor had dissipated so greatly that he could not even believe himself or his fabrications. And at times, he confessed, he didn't know the difference. He was losing his soul and his humanity. These painful revelations did not come easily.

It became clear that this client was suffering from major depression. He agreed to a psychiatric consultation and was medicated quickly and with excellent results. He stopped abusing alcohol, especially after he was read the riot act one day by an upper manager.

Yet medication and the threat of failure were not enough to empower this individual to truly invest himself in his recovery. Ultimately, through intense therapy, he was able to stop repressing his identity and to finally face moral accountability. His sense of well-being began to increase, and he began to heal. He was able to talk about his extreme fear of failure and his apprehension about maintaining or even remotely deserving his success.

He committed to a three-times-a-week treatment regimen. Inevitably, he began to restore his dignity by taking a fearless moral inventory of his life, his value system, his relationships, and his inner self. He began to build his gyroscope, thanks to which he could finally feel safe and whole.

We Already Know Right from Wrong

Modifying behavior to maintain the communal status quo is not enough, because deep down, we all know right from wrong. Even psychopaths know right from wrong, but they consider the distinctions irrelevant. When you deny your integrity, there are consequences. If you are not prepared to master yourself—your *self*—no matter how innovative the technique, you will fail. (This is the major flaw in the self-help industry. You simply cannot be satisfied while pursuing standards set by others if you are repressing you own moral instincts. On the surface, this may sound counterintuitive, coming from someone actually advocating a self-help regimen.)

However, in many instances, my clients need to fully understand concepts of morality and virtue in order to meaningfully apply them to themselves. Given the money-mad world in which financial professionals (FPs) work, you would be surprised how many struggle to simply define the term "virtue" or "morality," especially in the contemporary context. And so I often start at the beginning, clarifying and exploring the meanings of these concepts. It is after this exercise in emotional etymology that real progress can be made. No longer are they chasing someone else's standards, because they rediscover their own aspirations toward virtue.

Most people *do* want to know right from wrong as well as practice that knowledge. That is why I contend that The Wall Street Psychologist's Gyroscope is driven by self-awareness, introspection, self-examination, and a fearless inventory of your inner life. As well as the courage to reveal yourself. Let us explore some of these terms, starting with the one that is consistently the most difficult to decipher:

Reacquainting Yourself with Morality

Unfortunately, our culture's concepts of morality and virtue have been usurped. Contrary to Aristotle's teachings, for too many people, especially those in the financial services industry, it is now the accumulation of wealth for the sake of wealth that is the primary objective. Today, men and women born penniless can work hard and become the wealthiest among us. Yet rich or poor, ancient Greek or modern-day American, it is not simply "nice" to have money.

Money is, simply put, a stark necessity of life in a society. Without money we cannot shelter or feed ourselves or afford effective health care when we are injured or sick. And, for those of us fortunate enough to have more of it than what's needed just to survive, money makes life more comfortable and amusing, because we can afford higher-quality essentials, as well as toys, travel, and entertainment.

For many people, money serves as a powerful incentive to work hard, which in turn breeds good character, self-confidence, mental and physical fitness, and creativity. On a larger scale, money bankrolls important ideas and investments for the good of science, culture, and society. It encourages the ongoing exchange of valuable, life-enriching goods and services, which in turn generate employment opportunities. It protects, preserves, and delights us, and it enhances the way and extent to which we can exercise our freedoms.

In other words, money is good. But you already knew that. What you perhaps didn't know, or what you may need to learn a bit more about, is how to identify the circumstances in which money can be limiting—in which it ceases to contribute to feelings of autonomy, flexibility, and freedom and starts to mean something entirely different.

"The Good Life"—The Morality of Money and Wealth

As wealth increasingly came to be measured in terms of money, Aristotle made a profound observation that, 2,500 years later, still influences the financial markets. To Aristotle money represented exclusively the commodities it could buy. One can store wealth in the form of money, but money alone is not wealth, because he or she who has nothing but money starves. Money's power is in the value it can obtain. It is a medium of exchange by which people can accrue other components of wealth, which in ancient times included property, livestock, implements, and slaves. The more money one had, the more of these components he could buy for himself—not only to survive but also to flourish: to live comfortably but also morally. These are aspects of what Aristotle called "the good life" or eudaemonia.

This is a fascinating departure from previous conceptions of money, as Aristotle advocated the accumulation of wealth, not as an end in itself but as a way of attaining a more fulfilling life experience. Money was seen as a conduit to the pursuit of pleasure—righteous pleasure that was in sync with morality. Virtue was also a component of *the good life,* defined by Aristotle as the harmony of the soul in compliance with virtue, both intellectual and moral. Money represented the collective resources to achieve such harmony.

"Would You Put Your Mother in It?"

"The love of money is the root of all evil."—Paul (1 Timothy, 6: 7–10)

"Lack of money is the root of all evil."—George Bernard Shaw

"So you think money is the root of all evil. Have you ever asked what is the root of all money?"—Ayn Rand (1905 to 1982)

"Would you put your mother in it?"—Anonymous

Money = Complicated. No one ever said reconciling the moral implications of dealing in money with life in the financial world would be easy. Whether or not they are a subject of conversation or buried in the recesses of the minds of dealmakers, ethics play a role in every decision, every trade, every conversation, every smidgen of profit, and every loss. One retail broker with whom I had worked for years often talked about "end-of-the-month" ethics. At these junctures, just as most of his colleagues, he was confronted with a tough choice: whose life was it anyway, and whose interest should come first? He asserted that "the letter of the law vis-à-vis fiduciary responsibility" was tough to handle, especially at the end of the month, when he was publicly compared to his colleagues and to his own annualized production.

On Wall Street they even have a clever litmus test they use to gauge integrity—from the details of the largest deals to the toxicity of the smallest tips on the trading floor.

"Would you put your mother in it?"

Now, lest there should be any ambiguity, let it be made clear that mothers are sacred entities who warrant reverence and protection in all matters of state and commerce, in private and public life! In my experience treating hundreds of FPs from all strata of the Street, for those who lack moral rigor, the prevailing posture is less a malicious intent to harm than a self-serving ambivalence toward morality. But, as on the playground, on the Street you *do not* mess with anyone's mother.

An Environment Not Conducive to Morality

Under ideal circumstances, most people I treat would be less likely to shed their morality. Sadly, the financial services industry is not an environment conducive to maintaining morality.

It is an environment driven by a certain sense of oblivious bravado, such as the one described by many young FPs I've counseled, who openly acknowledged opening accounts and recruiting new clients under suspect conditions. They were desperate to do something, anything, to get into the market and frequently misled gullible clients, who were ready to buy anything they sold because these clients trusted them: their financial advisor, their wealth manager. Titles are big on the Street—they're supposed to be: designed to impress.

It is a cycle of voracious appetites, with the FP selling, selling, selling; preying on the client's greed, lucky as long as market gains are masking his poor performance. The broker, in turn, is a victim of the whims of his manager, locked in his own desperate, daily power struggle with the top management "downtown." In one breath FPs brag of their latest score or bet, while in the next they complain that their managers are constantly badgering them to sell a new product, a new financial instrument, a new stock. Some will jump from firm to firm, dragging accounts with them, often garnering good signing bonuses in the process.

One client I counseled was prepared to literally put her own cousin in any investment. In fact, during sessions she seethed about how she hated her cousin and revealed how she wanted to squander the contents of the account she managed for him, hasten his financial and, ultimately, physical demise, and fight his children over a $1-million savings account he allowed her to manage for him. Her cousin was ill for years, and put his entire trust in her. I had to discharge this client; her psychopathy was out of control.

The High Price of Immorality

Morality in the financial services industry is a scarce, incredibly dear resource. Professionals are beset by an endless cycle of ethical skirmishes, with many resigning themselves to the conclusion: "I cannot afford to be moral, and if anyone tells you they can, they're lying." Yet what they do not understand is that with each instance of compromising their character, they surrender a bit more of their integrity. Unbeknownst to them, there are consequences to these moral sacrifices.

Fraud and deception statistics are startling. The number of claims filed by investors concerning stockbroker fraud and other breaches of fiduciary duty escalated significantly in 2009, according to statistics[1] released by the Financial Regulatory Authority (FINRA),[2] which regulates more than 5,000 brokerage firms in the United States. The number of claims by investors seeking to recover losses is estimated at over 7,000 for this year. By comparison, there were only 4,982 securities fraud arbitration claims filed for the entire year in 2008 and 3,238 filed in 2007.[3] Many additional claims are never filed owing to avoidance, laziness, fear, paranoia, marginal thinking, denial, and so on.

In April 2009, lobbyists for investment planner professionals submitted a request to congressional lawmakers to create a national regulatory body to oversee their industry and establish industrywide standards. At that point in time, almost anyone could claim to be a financial planner and did not need to be credentialed as a Certified Financial Planner.

---

[1] https://www.finra.org/arbitration-mediation/dispute-resolution-statistics

[2] FINRA is a nongovernmental regulatory body that handles the resolution of disputes between investors and stockbrokers and other financial firms. It was created in July 2007 as a successor to the National Association of Securities Dealers to arbitrate stockbroker fraud claims that can include charges of breach of contract, breach of fiduciary duty, negligence, misrepresentation, unauthorized trading, and other claims that investments were improperly handled.

[3] According to online researcher AboutLawsuits.com, Not only are there more claims, but more claimants are finding success in their investor arbitration cases, which may be attributable to new SEC rules enacted at the beginning of the year that restrict defendants' ability to file a motion to dismiss. The rule was designed so that more claimants' cases would receive hearings on their merits and to prevent defendants from attempting to delay hearings, increasing costs for investors and generally intimidating them out of arbitration.

Meanwhile, Kroll's Global Fraud Report 2008[4] found that the average large U.S. company surveyed had lost approximately $8.2 million to fraud within the previous 3 years, with 85 percent of the companies polled suffering at least one instance of fraud during that time frame. That same year, the 2008 Report to the Nations[5] by the Association of Certified Fraud Examiners estimated that the real cost of fraud and worker embezzlement is equivalent to 7 percent of a company's annual revenue. These are astounding findings.

So-called "white-collar crime" is nothing new. The idea of white-collar crime was first discussed by researcher and author Edwin Sutherland during an address at a meeting of the American Sociological Association in 1939. In his book *White Collar Crime*, Sutherland explains that "... white collar crime may be defined approximately as a crime committed by a person of respectability and high social status in the course of his occupation."[6]

More recently, a report to the U.S. Department of Justice entitled "The Measurement of White-Collar Crime Using Uniform Crime Reporting (UCR) Data" revealed that from 1997 through 1999 white-collar crime accounted for nearly 4 percent of all incidents reported to the FBI, including such transgressions as computer crime, embezzlement, counterfeiting/forgery, insider trading, and other fraud offenses. Regarding warning signs, Embezzlement Warning Signs, an article on FindLaw.com, reports that red flags are almost as numerous as the tactics, including unbalanced accounts, unexplained losses, missing documents, altered checks, payments to false accounts, and delayed bank deposits.

Lack of Morality Breeds Mistrust

For all the good there is in money, there is also its flip side. Money does not guarantee happiness, self-esteem, pride, achievement, or emotional intimacy. Money does not necessarily correlate with integrity or honor. Money can be an instrument of creation, a creative tool, but when you

---

[4]Kroll Fraud & Embezzlement Investigations; www.kroll.com.

[5]http://www.acfe.com/rttn.aspx.

[6]E. Sutherland. 1939. *White Collar Crime* (New York, NY: Holt, Rinehart & Winston), p. 9.

become obsessed with it to the extent that you judge yourself and other people only by the portfolio value, sacrificing all spirit and sense of self, money ceases to be a source for good.

By dint of their trade, Wall Street professionals become experts at taking other people's financial inventory. They judge other people's worth and assess their value as a person by the volume of their holdings. This type of thinking can only limit an individual's scope, and ultimately his ability to be creative and effective with his clients, managers, and his employees and partners.

In fact, these types of people become so conditioned to value consumption and materialism above all else that they often do not realize the full degree of their one-track obsession—or even the fact of its existence. They will deny their obsessive behavior, even in the face of it. Money can make people think they have control and power over themselves and others, but all too often this is a delusion on their part. You can have all the money in the world yet still not be in control of your health or your relationships, your family's well-being, or your emotional and intellectual fulfillment.

At times this is hard to remember, when, in a professional environment everyone's perceived value seems to be based on production—how much money the individual generates for the company—the size of the office, the office view, the parking space, the alliances, the title, the number of assistants, the base compensation and the bonus, and even the number of telephone lines. The one-upmanship never ends.

In this kind of environment, it's easy to fall into the mindset that measures personal value, self-worth, and soul content by production, and production alone. After all, what else is there in an industry that seems purely focused on making money, as a function of production? Production is a mechanical term; does it really reflect the toil and dedication that good FPs actually manifest?

Within The Wall Street Psychologist's Gyroscope, other possibilities exist, such as justified pride, a sense of accomplishment, personal integrity, and even (on occasion) recognition. The problem is that Production Is King is so ingrained in Street culture that it has become a standard and a code of "righteous" behavior. In such an environment there can be little trust but much suspicion, corruption, and collusion. Why else would they feel compelled to ask, "Would you put your mother in it?"

Morality Cleanses the Psyche

Money may empower people, but its inherent polarities can also contribute to a sense of imprisonment. Obsession with money can breed greed, paranoia, fear, delusions of elitism and superiority, and envy. Conversely, inching toward morality in your thoughts helps incrementally free yourself from such corrupting negativity.

When you have to ask a question such as "Would you put your mother in it?" you surrender all trust, both externally and internally, as you concede your voluntary role in this never-ending quest for money. Deep inside, you know there are few people you can trust, just as you know you cannot be trusted at times.

There are consequences to breaking social contracts. Viewing money as a be-all-and-end-all can be isolating and constricting, because money cannot substitute for a healthy and happy sense of self. Morality and trust build, create. Lack of morality and lack of trust erode, destroy. If not kept in perspective, money can create emotional incarceration.

FPs, in particular, often exhibit codependency problems: their sense of self-worth, both in and out of work, is nearly entirely dependent on their job performance. I am reminded of a Wall Street trader years ago. He was wildly successful, accumulating millions in cash, with no debt. However, he suffered with demons from his youth: he never felt adequate, he always felt less than. He went on buying sprees, the more expensive the object, the better, but the sense of emptiness and inadequacy never went away.

He ultimately decompensated, lost most of his money, and then—and only then—was he able to begin to work toward some semblance of balance and sanity. Only then was he able to see and process without fear what he really thought and felt. Over time, he was able to recoup most of his holdings. He tempered his lifestyle. He sold off his "collections" and embraced humility.

I do not preach a brand of bland existence or a blindly altruistic approach to buying, selling, trading, or asset management. That could be tantamount to professional and financial suicide for many in finance. It is critical that you cultivate ways to apply moral principles that do not threaten you and also learn to compartmentalize personal values.

Compartmentalization, after all, is a necessary mechanism of defense and survival.

Money is not inherently bad. Clearly, it is what you do with money that defines its perceived morality, goodness, and function, in concert with its origins, that is, how you made it. Money can be utilized as a creative tool in so many different ways.

We certainly admire Bill Gates and Warren Buffet, who we believe earned their money honestly and in a way that did not exclude the enhancement of other aspects of their lives, actually including the enhancement of the lives of others via their global-scale philanthropy. But we certainly don't admire credit abusers and Ponzi scam artists for the greed and nefarious ways in which they pursue wealth to the point of creating profound pain, loss, and even complete demise for the many people they swindle. True success is about honesty, integrity, and balance: the effective balancing of multiplying money with the practice of core human virtues—love, trust, pride, and honor. Ultimately, a sound Gyroscope must encapsulate these principles. And your mother would be quite proud.

Morality, Respect, Integrity, Dignity

Morality is all around us, if we want to see it, if we want to believe in it. It manifests itself in the small gestures, deeds, and private thoughts that exemplify the very best of humanity. It is in our lives, in how we strive, in our books and in our films, in our relationships, and in our aspirations. The darkness can give way to the light. Life need not be a downward spiral.

When I think of the conflict between morality and money, I think of works such as *The Way of the Samurai*, Yukio Mishima's version of the Hagakure, an 18th-century practical and spiritual guide for the Japanese warrior. Mishima knowingly writes of the "expense account aristocrat" in reference to a man who has trouble telling the difference between his own money and that of his lord (*Way of the Samurai* Melville 1967).

He writes: "Dignity is the outward manifestation of inviolable self-respect; it is what makes a man a man" and:

Set your sights on honor and wealth. A samurai who has no interest in wealth or honor usually ends up a petty human being, slandering others. Such a man is vain and useless and in the end proves inferior to a man who is ambitious for wealth and fame. He is of no immediate practical use.

These are wise words not only for the samurai but for FPs too. The progressive Wall Street professional respects his client's money and its sanctity. He never underestimates his clients' dignity. You are in the business of creating and managing wealth; it is your life's work, but your own well-being must come first, which means you must also be effective at managing and taking proper care of yourself.

This brings us to a final observation from Mishima: "There is always room for improvement. A samurai's training lasts a lifetime." In my experience treating Wall Street professionals for 30 years, the best and ultimately happiest of my clients always bear the following in mind: there are always new things to learn, new ways to sharpen one's skills and intelligence, and leading a well-balanced and fulfilling life is both a process and an end in itself.

The Importance of Character

The raison d'être of this section is to provide the modern business professional with the context for developing and maintaining an effective Gyroscope that will facilitate long-term success and satisfaction. Easier said than done.

In his book *Crisis of Character: Building Corporate Reputation in the Age of Skepticism* (Firestein 2009),[7] a revealing examination of "how the psychology and culture of corporate life determine both short- and long-term business outcomes," author Peter Firestein introduces a series of original concepts, including the concept of "structural corruption," defined as "a condition, often within an industry, in which standard operating procedure is unethical, imposing difficult choices on well-meaning managers."

---

[7]P. Firestein. 2009. *Crisis of Character: Building Corporate Reputation in the Age of Skepticism* (New York, NY: Union Square Press).

What is particularly striking about Firestein's perspective is how he captures the evolving requisites of effective corporate leadership. Previously, as the author explains, senior leadership was accustomed to applying proven best practices to the pursuit of specific goals. This metrics-based approach to performance, though, in a way, necessary, suffers from a rigidity that leaves the corporate leader ill-equipped to address complex, ambiguous situations. Therefore, today's leader needs to supplement the business methodology with a custom approach informed by life experience and personal traits.

It would seem that this is common sense, yet in an environment where measurable results drive decisions, integrity is often the casualty of pragmatism. The ability to hit tangible targets is now as important as the capacity to manage the less tangible components of reputation to advance business strategies. If you do not have a firm grasp of the concepts of character, this is certainly a slippery slope, especially in light of the intense scrutiny of analysts, investors, the media, and government.

How Do You Define Your Character?

When reviewing this section, think about how you would respond to incidences of the structural corruption Firestein (2009) describes. Think about what character means to you. Think about virtue. Think about integrity. Character is a good place to start, whether you are defining or redefining yourself as a Wall Street FP. Character has many common definitions, but I prefer to define the term as:

1. the aggregate of traits forming the individual nature of a person;
2. moral or ethical quality;
3. reputation;
4. an accounting of the qualities and peculiarities of a person.

In psychology and psychoanalysis, however, character has other meanings. It is the evaluation of a person's moral qualities. Character implies attributes including integrity, courage, loyalty, and fortitude. Character is derived from the Greek sense of the idea. Character was originally used as a mark impressed on a coin, and Aristotle said that character implied moral virtue or excellence. Abraham Lincoln said: "Character is like a tree and reputation like its shadow. The shadow is what we think of it; the tree is the real thing."

Psychologists contend that character is a system of relatively fixed motivational traits that are demonstrated when an individual interacts with other people. And what about you? How do you define character? How do you define your character? My experience with clients has been that the best answers are given not in terms of the professional that we see, but of the one he or she aspires to be. After all, aspirations for personal integrity and professional virtue form the essence of The Wall Street Psychologist's Gyroscope.

CHAPTER 4

A New Way to Interpret Old Theories: Smith, Marx, Keynes

In the financial services industry, ignorance is far from bliss. Uninformed, you are at the mercy of others. When you merely regurgitate their opinions, you accept a state of subservience. Conversely, thinking for yourself is empowering. Now, this goes much deeper than simply learning the tips and tricks of the trade. Your ability to interpret core economic theories and utilize them to form your core ideology is critical for your empowerment. How to approach it? Well, you know yourself better than anyone else can or ever will. I'm here just to show the way and to guide you on the path.

A career in the financial services is not just a job; it is a calling requiring a full immersion in a culture. This is why in my practice I encourage clients to invest the time, educate themselves on as many schools of theory as possible, and to fully commit to the process of psychoanalysis. From the fires of that analysis typically emerges a financial professional (FP) with a firmer footing and reduced anxiety, depression, and a host of psychological ills stemming from ignorance. The technique I practice to soothe the anxiety and helplessness my clients experience is, essentially, *psychological enlightenment through intellectual and emotional empowerment.*

The Human Evolution of Economic Theory

In the previous section we established some of the historical context relevant to the development of the financial markets and their influence on our values and culture. Our intention here is not to recap financial history, as other writers have done this more comprehensively. Rather, the objective in selecting certain historical milestones is to provide a backdrop for a more robust exploration of the psychology of money.

Because money is so ingrained in the DNA of the human experience—the latter seen as a materialist distillation, if you will, of the human condition—it is an ever-present element of the modern Western human mind. Because one can never fully excise the fallibility of humanity from economics, the purpose of this section is to continue along our trajectory and examine what I call the Human Evolution of Economic Theory.

We will not exhaustively weigh the merits of modern economic theory, but will rather discuss select economic developments that highlight key categories of psychological influence. We begin this discussion with a review of some of the better-known economic theorists: Adam Smith, John Maynard Keynes, Karl Marx. With the luxury of hindsight, we explore how their theories either worked in sync or conflicted with our natural human instincts and collective behavior. We apply elements of this discussion to the role of the FP, ideally providing the context my target audience can use to best process the guidance I provide in my program. Last, we reinterpret the teachings of two master manipulators—Niccolò Machiavelli and Sun Tzu—so often quoted and so little understood in financial circles, as the true value in interpreting their work is not necessarily in adopting ruthless tactics, but rather in understanding how to apply selective pragmatism.

Over 30 years of professional practice, I have found that despite their superior intelligence, my clients have difficulty gaining perspective on their lives. Their specific experience, as anyone else's, may be unique, but the machinations of the financial services industry that cause them such grief are certainly not. The FPs I treat often become helplessly inured to the darker corners of the industry, seduced by vast riches, coerced by greed and power, forced into fraught decisions and moral sacrifices.

My aim is to empower the reader with knowledge of the psychology of money, the better to be able to establish their internal *Gyroscope* to survive the seductions of vice and to prosper in every sense in a money-mad world.

Accepting the Inevitability of Disaster

In his book, *The Ascent of Money*, Niall Ferguson documents the financial history of the world. Ferguson contends that finance is the foundation of human progress and maintains that financial history is the "essential back-story behind all history. The evolution of credit and debt was as important as any technological innovation in the rise of civilization, from ancient Babylon to the silver mines of Bolivia," he writes. "Banks provided the material basis for the splendor of the Italian Renaissance, while the bond market was the decisive factor in conflicts from the Seven Years' War to the American Civil War."

Ferguson goes on to aptly point out what is perhaps the most salient financial truth around: "Yet the most important lesson of financial history is that sooner or later every bubble bursts; sooner or later the bearish sellers outnumber the bullish buyers; sooner or later greed flips into fear." If, as history demonstrates, financial markets are inevitably subject to such boom-and-bust cyclicality, and if the tone of our culture is so integrated into the economic state, why must we suffer so?

Why have we not evolved to the point where we have at least minimized the potential for massive financial catastrophe? Why, in 2009, did the threat of another Great Depression, poised to surpass that of the Depression of the 1930s, almost come to be? Why do we make the same mistakes? Is it possible that our economic theorists and philosophers are *that* misguided and myopic in their speculations?

In his essay, *Beyond the Pleasure Principle* (1920), Sigmund Freud contended that people repeat traumatic events over and over again. This type of reliving represents an attempt at mastery and control. According to neo-Freudians, corrective emotional experiences can repair the trauma. History keeps repeating itself so that we could learn from mistakes and correct our behavior in order to achieve stability and security—both peace of mind and a piece of the pie. And yet if we do not learn from our mistakes over this cycle of repeats, there is obviously a masochistic element to this process.

On Wall Street, it appears that the envelope is always being pushed to its bursting point, because people want to squeeze the most out of any product or service in order to maximize profit and gain, thereby threatening the elasticity of the actual membrane of any bubble. My purpose in writing this book is not to dispel, nor even to debate, the concepts of Ferguson, Freud, or any other authority. Both my practice and my prose are aimed at enabling the individual to cope with crisis, to survive, and to grow. To get there, I encourage the reader to reexamine key concepts, not from financial or economic perspectives, but through the lens of psychology and, to an extent, sociology.

When you learn to look at the psychological factors and influences behind market dynamics, you have a more comprehensive knowledge base from which to draw informed conclusions.

What Would Adam Smith Say Today?

No book addressing the intersection of economics and psychology would be complete without a discussion of Adam Smith, the father of modern economics. Smith (1723–1790), a Scots philosopher, is considered the founder of modern economic theory. Possessing infinite faith in humanity, Smith believed that people would act in their own self-interest while producing the goods or services required by society. Somewhat of a poet, Smith contended that an "invisible hand" was the mechanism behind this self-regulation. His magnum opus, *The Wealth of Nations*, was published in the year of the proclamation of independence by a country that, arguably, took both the poetry and the call to action in his philosophy most directly and diligently to heart.

Smith felt that a free-market economy could run on its own steam, on autopilot, as it were. His key concept supported a *laissez-faire* attitude (the French term literally means "let do," as in "leave it be") by the powers that be, i.e., the government, although Smith never actually used that term. In essence, he felt that the market would take care of itself, believing in harmony and growth, as well as being an outspoken opponent of government intervention, product regulation, trade restrictions, and labor laws.

This metaphor of the invisible hand, also known as "the invisible hand of the market," coined by Smith in *The Theory of Moral Sentiments*, is a fascinating allegory of what he saw as the self-regulating nature of the marketplace. For Smith, the invisible hand was the concomitance of the forces of self-interest, competition, supply, and demand, which, he noted, would be capable of allocating resources in society. I, liberally, refine this theory to suggest that there are many invisible hands competing and collaborating to shape and reshape our economic landscape and, ultimately, our existence.

Mired in the Muck of Credit Defaults "Swamps"

One wonders what Adam Smith would say about credit default swaps (CDS). At first blush, a CDS seems like a financial instrument with every reason for being; essentially, it represents an insurance policy on a bond. An investor purchases bonds issued by Acme Corp. with the expectation of receiving periodic payments, say, every 6 months. However, there is a likelihood that Acme Corp. may go bankrupt and default on those bonds. This may represent a minimal risk, yet if it comes to pass, the investor will no longer receive the regular payments. Therefore, the investor may opt to purchase a CDS as a kind of insurance policy. If Acme Corp. doesn't go bankrupt, the investor absorbs the expense of the CDS, or the premium on the insurance policy that it, in essence, is. Should Acme Corp. indeed go bankrupt, the investor will receive a payout, per the terms of the CDS.

This seems like a responsible way of managing risk, an outgrowth and qualification of the process of lending money to finance growth, and one that Mr. Smith would likely endorse, at least as a concept. But let's say it becomes increasingly difficult to earn a return on traditional investment vehicles. So rather than specialize on trading bonds, with their minimal rates of return, more and more entities start to sell CDS instruments.

The risk, at least historically, seems low, there is no up-front cash outlay, and you only have to pay out if the issuer defaults, which they rarely do. Besides, you can always borrow to pay down your obligations, right? This is why, beginning in the 1990s, banks and hedge funds began to more aggressively buy and sell CDS contracts, as opposed to the actual bonds. By the end of 2007, the global market for CDS contracts had grown to approximately $60 trillion.

Unfortunately, many of these CDS contracts were insurance policies on exotic, complex financial instruments that powered a massive buildup in subprime lending. As those mortgage-backed securities and collateralized debt obligations imploded—as they were basically bundles of bad loans that should never have been extended in the first place—the banks and hedge funds were faced with the grim prospect of honoring those CDS contracts.

As most banks bought *and* sold CDS contracts, a default would not produce a net change. They paid out on defaults, but also collected. There were some, however, who only sold CDS contracts. AIG was one such financial institution. It sold $440 billion in CDS contracts and subsequently required a massive $85-billion federal bailout, as the subprime mortgage and banking crisis plunged the global economy into a deep recession. I wonder how Smith would apply his theories to this debacle.

Well, actually, there are elements of Smith's argument that are applicable, especially when it comes to limiting government intrusion into the markets. But, again, I do not intend to debate the merits of Smith's theories, or any other philosopher's tenets, for that matter. Rather, my point is that not every link in the chain that was wrapped around the throat of the global economy during the subprime-lending and subsequent banking crises was solely the product of short-sighted economic policies.

The force tightening the chain was human folly and a psychology grounded in greed. Subprime loans were cavalierly extended to—even aggressively foisted upon—borrowers who in turn made their own irresponsible decisions, taking on major, long-term debt to finance new homes and automobiles without the financial wherewithal to repay it. Lenders dangled enticing incentives before naïve borrowers in a mad race to drive up the volume of loan originations, which in turn paid hefty commissions.

Brokers hid the true performance of these bad loans in collateralized pools that were supposed to aggregate the risk yet were often not properly valued. Bankers created a growing array of financial instruments to derive even more commissions from the trading of these pools of bad loans, including CDS contracts. Government regulators either did not understand or were irresponsible in oversight and did not adequately protect the investing public. Investors sank fortunes into the market, thus enabling and propagating a dangerous herd mentality.

The Dangerous Illusion of Value

This cycle of greed was based on an illusion of value, driven and magnified by natural market dynamics. In hindsight it is easy for some to say that the events in question should have been anticipated and foreknown, but the fact is that no one was able to halt this juggernaut from nearly destroying our financial markets.

Again, the previously mentioned Fatal Flaw Theory: "If something seems too good to be true, it probably is." And if history has taught us anything, it is that this is not the last market disaster. In fact, the National Bureau of Economic Research (NBER) estimates that there have been as many as 47 recessions[1] in the United States since the Panic of 1797 (precipitated, fittingly enough, by the bursting of a land-speculation bubble).

Why are so many people willing to perpetuate such dysfunctional market dynamics? As an FP, how do you avoid being sucked down the rabbit hole? Of course, involving Adam Smith in a conversation regarding CDS contracts and banking disasters more than two centuries after his death may be seen as merely an intellectual exercise. However, it is no more senseless than financial media pundits applying stoic economic theories to explain market machinations, while neglecting to devote equal weightage to psychological influences.

Our obsession with the concept of money and its many facets has influenced virtually every major event in our modern evolution. Niall Ferguson is correct in his premise that financial history is the de facto history of humanity. Ultimately, understanding The Wall Street Psychologist's Gyroscope requires an appreciation of the psychology of this solid bond and a reconciliation of it with applicable economic principles.

There are many different schools of economic thought, and each revolutionary theorist was right to a significant extent, especially in regard to his particular moment in history and geography. As a result, today we enjoy a pluralistic model, adaptable to many different situations as they arise. Interpret the words of each master of economics within the context

---

[1]The NBER defines a recession as "a significant decline in economic activity spread across the economy, lasting more than a few months, normally visible in real gross domestic product (GDP), real income, employment, industrial production, and wholesale-retail sales."

of their argument. If such context is absent, seek it out and interpret it for yourself within the context of the current situation.

Unlocking Keynes' Theories

John Maynard Keynes (1883 to 1946) is another master of economic theory highly relevant to The Wall Street Psychologist's Gyroscope. More than a half-century before the "Too-Big-to-Fail" bank bailouts of the U.S. banking industry, Keynes advocated interventionist economic policy, encouraging governments to leverage fiscal and monetary policies to allay the adverse consequences of downturns in business cycles, economic recessions, and depressions. His ideas form the basis for the school of thought known as Keynesian economics, and its derivatives.

Essentially, Keynes argued that decisions made by individuals and groups in the private sector at times produce negative macroeconomic results that may be mitigated by monetary measures and policy actions in the public sector.[2]

Whereas classical economists argue for the validity of Say's Law— "supply creates its own demand"—as a market mechanism for avoiding "general gluts," Keynes posited that the collective demand for goods might be deficient in times of economic crisis, fueling high unemployment and restricting output. Thus, Keynes contended, government policies should be applied to enhance the aggregate demand, thereby spurring economic growth and decreasing unemployment and deflation.

Keynes' strategy for recovering from a depression was to stimulate the economy by reducing interest rates and increasing government investment in infrastructure. As did any economic theorist of substance, Keynes had his detractors, although his theories were widely embraced by Western economic powers in the wake of World War II, and we have seen tactics based on them wielded with varying success in successive depressions and recessions ever since.

Understanding Keynes also involves appreciating his emphasis on the creation and coordination of international economic institutions, and

---

[2]The theories forming the basis of Keynesian economics were first presented in *The General Theory of Employment, Interest and Money*, published in 1936 by John Maynard Keynes.

the degree to which economic developments influence social events, such as war and peace. In his 1919 bestseller, *The Economic Consequences of the Peace*, Keynes objected to the harshly punitive reparation payments imposed on Germany by the Allied powers after the end of World War I. He rightfully assessed that the amounts were so exorbitant that Germany would remain perpetually poor and politically unstable. Unfortunately, his prescience was accurate, ultimately producing the disasters that were the rise of the Nazi Party and World War II.

Studying Keynes, one gains an appreciation of the labyrinthine manner in which the economic stratum of society is intertwined with its political and social fabric. The markets do not operate in a vacuum, and the savvy FP must be aware of the entire scope of the market's influence and the degree to which markets are subject to intervention.

When a broker adopts a particular strategy, he must think beyond its immediate impact and survey the larger political and social stage in order to adjust the execution. For instance, subprime lending was facilitated, in part, by the prevalent ideology of mass homeownership. Subsequently, many loans were originated that should not have been, putting thousands of Americans in homes they really could not afford. When those loans hit Wall Street, bundled into pools of mortgage-backed securities, many different ways to trade their value were devised, including complex derivative strategies that many traders simply did not understand. This was a setup for failure.

In hindsight, the fallout was inevitable, but few actually managed to get out of the way. A better student of economic history would have looked beyond the balance sheet and analyzed trading in subprime lending more comprehensively. Applying Keynesian theory, they would have sensed the inevitability of the government's intervention, albeit applied selectively, as Lehman Brothers learned. Critics of Keynes would note the backlash at the government bailouts now evident, and the increased scrutiny now placed on public companies, especially in the area of compensation.

Ultimately, when incorporating Keynesian theory into the strategic engine of The Wall Street Psychologist's Gyroscope, the value is in anticipating the inevitability of intervention. In common parlance, the divide between Wall Street and Main Street is symbolic. As Keynes knew, both physically and psychologically, they are parts of the same thoroughfare.

Let's Not Forget Marx

This is not a comprehensive economic text, and I have chosen to highlight two giants in the field, Adam Smith and John Maynard Keynes. There are yet many different schools of economic theory and many derivatives of those schools. There are even some that capitalists wish never existed, some about as different from Smith as one can imagine.

Karl Heinrich Marx (1818 to 1883) was a German philosopher, political economist, historian, political theorist, sociologist, communist, and revolutionary, whose ideas are credited as being the foundation of modern communism. He is cited as much as, if not more than, Smith, and certainly more than Keynes.

In many ways, communism is the antithesis of capitalism, and it is precisely for this reason that the well-rounded money-minder should have at least a casual understanding of Marx's insights into the markets and the influence his theories have had on economic thinking. Having an informed viewpoint means you have reviewed all contextual sources and formed your own opinion. This is the essence of psychological empowerment through enlightenment.

Marx summarized his approach in the first line of chapter one of The Communist Manifesto, published in 1848: "The history of all hitherto existing society is the history of class struggles." Marx argued that capitalism, like previous socioeconomic systems, would inevitably produce internal tensions, which would lead to its demise. Just as capitalism replaced feudalism, he believed socialism would, in turn, replace capitalism and lead to a classless society in which struggles and rewards were shared and everyone contributed what they could and received what they needed. This would be called pure communism and would emerge after a transitional period called the "dictatorship of the proletariat": a period sometimes referred to as the "workers' state" or "workers' democracy."

I know... Such musings make most FPs shudder. But, then again, along that trajectory, you had Adam Smith, who believed that a free-market economy could run under its own steam, on automatic pilot. Keynes then advocated for strategic intervention to address crises. And Marx proposed eliminating capitalism in favor of a socialist society.

These three figures were polarizing, providing theories that have been subsequently wildly extrapolated and manipulated to suit different purposes. Yet within the complex folds of these sources you can draw out points to support your own empowerment. Within the confines of these theories lies your reality. Broadening your intellectual horizons can only enable you to develop your own sound theories and be better at your craft. How, you ask?

What Would Adam Smith Do?

Here is an exercise in altered reality. I recommend to the FP that, in an effort to expand his or her perspective, the FP assume the mindset of Smith, Keynes, and Marx and then run some hypothetical investment scenarios, focusing on the choice of companies in which these intellectuals would have invested, the trends to which they would have been sensitive, the decisions they would have made. This would enable the FP to evaluate an event or opportunity from many different perspectives and then make a better-informed decision, producing a more thought-through, sophisticated, creative viewpoint.

Ultimately, the FP must have at least a rudimentary understanding of these schools of thought in order to appreciate how they are interpreted (or misinterpreted) by others and then make well-advised decisions that are more than mere reflections of the biases of others. The better educated the individual is in economic theory and history, the more good his decision making and planning will bring to his clients, his firm, and himself.

Although not quite as maligned as lawyers, practitioners of the financial arts have still long suffered a dubious reputation in our culture. Consider, for instance, the roundly negative, though certainly amusing, observations on money, the stock market, and stockbrokers that Mark Twain, that salt-of-the-earth master of irony and the vituperative arts, had to offer.

Embracing Integrity, Rediscovering Virtue

In *Mark Twain's Notebook*, on the subject of money, he wrote: "Some men worship rank, some worship heroes, some worship power, some worship God, and over these ideals they dispute and cannot unite—but they all worship money." In *Pudd'nhead Wilson's Calendar*, Twain pointed out a feature of the stock market: "October: this is one of the peculiarly dangerous months to speculate in stocks in. The others are July, January, September, April, November, May, March, June, December, August, and February."[3] In the same work Twain offered the equally droll line: "There are two times in a man's life when he should not speculate: when he can't afford it and when he can."

In his work *Daniel in the Lion's Den-And Out Again All Right*, published in *The California* in November 1864, Twain takes several clever swipes at stockbrokers:

> I consider that a broker goes according to the instincts that are in him, [sic] and means no harm, and fulfills his mission according to his lights, and has a right to live, and be happy in a general way, and be protected by the law to some extent, just as a better man. I consider that brokers come into the world with souls—I am satisfied they do; and if they wear them out in the course of a long career of stock-jobbing, have they not a right to come in at the eleventh hour and get themselves half-soled, like old boots, and be saved at last?

> "Daniel In the Lion's Den—And Out Again All Right." November 5, 1864. *The Californian.* http://www.twainquotes.com/Calif/18641105 .html

Twain and others have long taken their swipes at the denizens of the Street. And there may be some credence to their character assassinations. When one defines the concept of the Wall Street professional, should character, virtue, and integrity be requisite components of that definition?

The fundamental purpose of this book is to enable the reader to develop a sound Gyroscope as a means of facilitating long-term personal

---

[3]In fact, Wikipedia now documents the "Mark Twain Effect" as the phenomenon of stock returns in October being lower than in other months. The '29, '87, and '08 crashes occurred in the month of October. Seems Mark Twain was on to something.

and professional fulfillment. And so this book is not for everyone. Those who seek out my professional advice are not sinister, narcissistic financial psychopaths. They are well aware of their struggle with demons, which are manifestations of the fact that they have simply lost their way. That is why when they enter treatment, I start by asking my clients to see if they can detect semblances of character, virtue, and integrity within themselves and their background. We then build on these perspectives and engage in the treatment process.

A New Way to Look at an Old Profession

In previous sections we explored the history of money and financial systems, while interpreting the evolution of economic theory through the lens of a psychologist. Now we seek to define the modern Wall Street FP, based on my observations as a psychologist treating FPs for more than 30 years.

Included throughout the following observations, analyses, and guidance are dramatic, perhaps disturbing anecdotes. Unfortunately, these stories are all too real and represent the manifestations of a money-mad industry. In "What They Did Not Teach You in Business School," we start at the beginning—when the FP enters the industry—imploding myths and shattering expectations.

We then delve into what is perhaps the single most important—and far too often overlooked and abused—concept of adherence to fiduciary responsibility. This program is not an ethics course, but rather an exploration of the psychology behind key ideas; no concept is more integral to the soundness of The Wall Street Psychologist's Gyroscope than the concept of fiduciary responsibility. In a sense, it is the guidance system for the Gyroscope. Further on in this section we explore various archetypes and complexes, in order to provide the FP with an understanding of what to avoid. After all, being able to identify the warning signs of danger is one way to avoid disaster down the road.

We also work through the psychology of reputation, while dissecting the complex, convoluted, materialistic value system that drives the Street's collective conscious. Finally, I provide a detailed list of the most common mistakes brokers make based on personal observations of the clients in my practice.

Will You Embrace Change?

For more context, and to enrich your reading experience, I call your attention to a fascinating book by W. Randall Jones[4] (2009) *The Richest Man in Town—The Twelve Commandments of Wealth*. Jones reminds us that Darwin was right when he observed: "It is not the strongest of the species that survives, nor the most intelligent, but the ones who are most responsive to change" (Darwin 1859).[5] The founder of *Worth* magazine, Jones, appropriately enough, identifies the "Richest Man in Town" in 100 American cities and towns, ranging from household names like Bill Gates to the lesser-known Fred DeLuca, founder of Subway; from Bob Stiller, founder of Green Mountain Coffee, to Jorge Perez, real estate mogul and the most financially successful Latino man in the country. On the basis of these moguls' insights, Jones maps out his 12 commandments of wealth:

1. Seek Money for Money's Sake and Ye Shall *Not* Find—"Money will only come when you are doing the right thing in the right way," according to Randal Kirk.
2. Find Your Perfect Pitch—"Knowing others is intelligence; knowing yourself is true wisdom. Mastering others is strength; mastering yourself is true power," counsels the Tao Te Ching.
3. BYOB: Be Your Own Boss—"You don't get rich working for other people," says Phil Ruffin.
4. Get Addicted to Ambition—"If we did all the things we are capable of doing, we would literally astound ourselves," said Thomas Edison.
5. Wake Up Early—Be early—"The sun has not caught me in bed for fifty years," Thomas Jefferson used to say.
6. Don't Set Goals—Execute or Get Executed—"Vision without execution is hallucination"—food for thought from Thomas Edison.
7. Fail in Order to Succeed—"I've failed over and over and over again in my life. That's why I succeeded," said Michael Jordan. "If you are going through hell, keep going," Winston Churchill instructed.

---

[4] W.R. Jones. 2009. *The Richest Man in Town* (New York, NY: Business Plus).
[5] C. Darwin. 1859. *On the Origin of Species* (London, England: Routledge). The attribution of this quote to Darwin has been disputed; the substance, however, still stands.

8. Location Does Matter—"There is no greater success than hometown success," opined Buzz Oates.

9. Moor Yourself to Morals—"It takes twenty years to build a reputation and five minutes to ruin it. If you think about that, you'll do things differently"—wisdom from Warren Buffet.

10. Say Yes to Sales—"Nothing happens until something is sold," believes Joe Ricketts.

11. Borrow from the Best and the Worst—"I not only use all the brains that I have, but all that I can borrow," said Woodrow Wilson.

12. Never Retire—"Find something you truly love to do and retire for the rest of your life," was one of James Hartley Click, Sr.'s *Twelve Commandments of Wealth*.

Our psyches comprise the sum of so many parts. The foregoing guidance provided is actionable only when the reader is truly perceptive, when he or she is willing to work and grow in the process. These 12 perspectives vary in subject and substance, yet all are sincere and based on a set of common denominators: experience, careful thinking, and self-reflection. It also helps that they are rooted in honesty, perseverance, and dedication to excellence. These same virtues are, collectively, a driving component of my treatment regimens. This section is designed to help you begin to take small steps down the path to wellness of the mind and the body. Are you willing? Are you ready?

References

Aboutlawsuits.com. 2009. "Stockbroker Fraud Arbitration Claims Continue Sharp Increase over Last Year." https://www.aboutlawsuits.com/stockbroker-fraud-claims-continue-increase-4847/.

Bayer, C. 2013. "War Is Hell, Business Ain't: Applying Sun Tzu's 'The Art of War.'" http://www.thewallstreetpsychologist.com/recent_posts/war-is-hell-business-aint-applying-sun-tzusthe-art-of-war/.

Curtis, A. 2002. *"The Century of the Self" 240 minutes*. London, England: British Broadcasting Corporation.

Darwin, C. 1859. *On the Origin of Species*. London, England: John Murray.

D'Eprio, P., and M.D. Pinkowish. 1998. *What Are the Seven Wonders of the World?* New York, NY: First Anchor Books.

Finra. 2019. http://www.finra.org/ArbitrationMediation/AboutFINRADR/Statistics/index.htm.

Firestein, P. 2009. *Crisis of Character: Building Corporate Reputation in the Age of Skepticism*. New York, NY: Union Square Press.

Izzard, E. 1990. "Dress to Kill," *Spotify Video*, 90 mins. https://open.spotify.com/album/1KZ5UsNXZ1ActL1c6jt5MA#login

Jones, R. 2009. *The Richest Man in Town*. New York, NY: Business Plus.

Jost, J.T., and O. Hunyady. 2002. "The Psychology of System Justification and the Palliative Function of Ideology." *European Review of Social Psychology* 13, pp. 111–53.

Keynes, J.M. 1936. *The General Theory of Employment, Interest and Money*. London, England: Palgrave Macmillan.

Kroll. 2008. Global Fraud Report, accessed July 10, 2016. https://eiuperspectives.economist.com/sites/default/files/FraudReport_English-UK_Sept08_1.pdf

Malcolm, M.G. 2005. *Blink: The Power of Thinking without Thinking*. New York, NY: Little, Brown and Company.

Mcclean, B., & Nocera, J. 2010. *All the Devils are Here: The Hidden History of the Financial Crisis*. New York, NY: Portfolio.

McCumiskey, J. 2011. What is Money. *Positive Money*: Retrieved January 20, 2019 at. https://positivemoney.org/2011/05/what-is-money/.

Melville, J. P. 1967. *Way of the Samurai*. Paris, France: Filmel.

Santayana, G. 2005. "The Life of Reason." http://www.gutenberg.org/files/15000/15000-h/15000-h.htm.

Shaw, J.B. 1903. *Man and Superman: The Revolutionist's Handbook.* New York, NY: Heritage Press.

Shortman, J. 2010. "How Competitive Are Hedge Funds, and Are They a Help or a Hindrance in Driving the Economy Out of Recession?" Norwich Economics Papers. https://www.uea.ac.uk/documents/953219/967353/Shortman_J.pdf/4347dbcd-fbf4-4f73-9140-638354243fb9.

Sutherland, E. 1939. *White Collar Crime.* New York, NY: Holt, Rinehart & Winston.

Twain, M. 1894. *Pudd'nhead Wilson.* New York, NY: Charles L. Webster & Company.

Twain, M. 1864. "Daniel in the Lion's Den and Out Again All Right." *The Californian.* http://www.twainquotes.com/Calif/18641105.html.

Werner, H. 1951. *Comparative Psychology of Mental Development.* New York, NY: International Universities Press.

Wikipedia. 2019. *"Money",* Last Modified January 29, 2019. Money. Retrieved Jan 12, 2019 at https://en.wikipedia.org/wiki/Money.

About the Author

Dr. Christopher Bayer is a member of the American Psychological Association, the Manhattan Psychological Association, the New York State Psychological Association, the Psychoanalytic Society of the Postdoctoral Program at New York University (NYU), and the Inventors' Association of Manhattan. In addition, he has practiced as a professional, New York City (NYC)-based, psychologist and psychoanalyst since the early 1980s and has specialized in the treatment of executives (in the banking and securities industries) and their families. He is Board-Certified and a diplomate fellow of the International College of Prescribing Psychologists (1997), certified in the treatment of alcohol and other psychoactive substance-use disorders, and a Department of Motor Vehicles (DMV)-certified substance abuse treatment provider and evaluator.

Dr. Bayer is the creator of a highly lauded financial-literacy program for high school students, MoneyMind101, launched at the Dalton School, which has since been taught at several NYC schools and institutes, including The Birch Wathen Lenox School, The Chapin School, The New York Health Education and Awareness Drive, and the New York Life Money Management & Investment Seminar. He has appeared on numerous American and Canadian television and radio programs, including "After the Bell" on Fox Business News, Minnesota Public Radio with noted financial writer William Cohan, the Gary Null Progressive Commentary Radio Hour with noted film documentarian Joel Bakan, and CJAD's "On Call with Dr. Sydney Miller," sharing his psychological analysis of financial topics. Dr. Bayer has also been a forensic sex abuse consultant on major cases in elite NYC private schools (Poly Prep Country Day School, Brooklyn, and Horace Mann School, Riverdale).

His contributions to the field of psychology, and to topics related to finance and psychology, have been significant. His early training took place at Clark University in Worcester, Massachusetts—the first graduate school in the United States, and the only American university where Sigmund Freud lectured (*Freud and Carl Jung Lectures* 1909). After receiving the

Vineberg Research Prize in 1970, Dr. Bayer completed an intensive externship at the Marshfield Clinic (modeled after the Mayo Clinic) the following year and graduated with a master's degree in experimental psychology (1971) and a doctorate in clinical psychology (1975) from the University of Manitoba's APA-approved program.

In 1982, Dr. Bayer earned a Certificate of Specialization in psychotherapy and psychoanalysis from NYU's Postdoctoral Psychology Program and held multiple lectureships at various schools throughout the City of New York. Namely, he was an adjunct lecturer at the New York College of Osteopathic Medicine for 8 years, taught Dream Analysis at the Long Island Institute of Mental Health for 4 years, and lectured at the School of Social Work at Adelphi University, Molloy College, and the Henry George School of Social Science.

Since 1976, Dr. Bayer has had a clinical practice based in Syosset and Manhattan, New York, as part of which he has treated hundreds of clients, most of whom are FPs. His service to the profession spans several decades, beyond the grounds of his clinical practice, and into the universities and the financial and social services arena. For more than a decade, he served as the psychological consultant at the Highland Preparatory School. Dr. Bayer has been a clinical supervisor in Yeshiva University's Psychology Doctoral Program and has trained interns and residents in Hillside Hospital's Psychology Internship Program.

Dr. Bayer has worked in a variety of settings: psychiatric hospitals (state and private), correctional facilities, drug and alcohol rehabilitation units, correctional institutions, community mental health centers, and various court systems (family, supreme, and federal). Recently, Dr. Bayer became a board member of the Psychoanalytic Society at NYU's Postdoctoral Psychology Program. He has chaired multiple fora at professional conventions. For example, he has served as Chairman of the Board of Directors and, jointly, Director of Research at the Helping End Eating Disorders (HEED) Foundation; as a guest lecturer at Adelphi University; on the faculty of the Long Island Institute of Mental Health and on that of the New York College of Osteopathic Medicine and has held the post of Supervisor at the Yeshiva University Clinical Psychology Doctoral Program from 1996 to 2006, in addition to having held posts as consulting or staff psychologist at multiple hospitals, medical centers, and other organizations throughout the 1970s, 1980s, and 1990s. Most recently, Dr. Bayer has served as a forensic evaluator for the Nassau County Supreme Court, as well as a psychological testing evaluator and expert witness in multiple court cases.

Dr. Bayer has authored dozens of articles and presentations and has made significant contributions to topics in psychology, particularly in the area of financial psychology and money intelligence. He has been the driving force behind theshareholderactivist.com, known as "The Social Network for Investor Empowerment" listed on Harvard Law School's Forum on Corporate Governance and Financial Regulation. Additionally, Dr. Bayer is the founder of forensicpsychologystrategiesny.com, where, as an expert consultant to lawyers and accountants, he builds models of behavior for use in criminal cases and IRS offer-in-compromise cases geared to tax penalty abatement.

Index

OTHER TITLES IN OUR ECONOMICS AND PUBLIC POLICY COLLECTION

Jeffrey Edwards, North Carolina A&T State University, *Editor*

- *Understanding the Indian Economy from the Post-Reforms of 1991, Volume II: Anatomy of the Indian Economy* by Shrawan Kumar Singh
- *Understanding the Indian Economy from the Post-Reforms of 1991, Volume I: History, Evolution, and Growth* by Shrawan Kumar Singh
- *Business Liability and Economic Damages, Second Edition* by Scott D. Gilbert
- *The Economics of Online Gaming: A Player's Introduction to Economic Thinking* by Andrew Wagner
- *Global Sustainable Capitalism* by Marcus Goncalves, Mario Svigir and Harry Xia
- *Political Dimensions of the American Macroeconomy* by Gerald T. Fox
- *The Options Trading Primer: Using Rules-Based Option Trades to Earn a Steady Income* by Russell A. Stultz
- *A Guide to International Economics* by Shahruz Mohtadi
- *Foreign Direct Investment: The Indian Experience* by Leena Ajit Kaushal
- *Urban Development 2120* by Peter Nelson
- *Disaster Risk Management in Agriculture: Case Studies in South Asian Countries* by Huong Ha, Lalitha S. Fernando and Sanjeev Kumar Mahajan
- *The Option Strategy Desk Reference: An Essential Reference for Option Traders* by Russell A. Stultz
- *Disaster Risk Management: Case Studies in South Asian Countries* by Huong Ha, Lalitha S. Fernando and Sanjeev Kumar Mahajan
- *Economic Renaissance In the Age of Artificial Intelligence* by Apek Mulay

Concise and Applied Business Books

The Collection listed above is one of 30 business subject collections that Business Expert Press has grown to make BEP a premiere publisher of print and digital books. Our concise and applied books are for…

- Professionals and Practitioners
- Faculty who adopt our books for courses
- Librarians who know that BEP's Digital Libraries are a unique way to offer students ebooks to download, not restricted with any digital rights management
- Executive Training Course Leaders
- Business Seminar Organizers

Business Expert Press books are for anyone who needs to dig deeper on business ideas, goals, and solutions to everyday problems. Whether one print book, one ebook, or buying a digital library of 110 ebooks, we remain the affordable and smart way to be business smart. For more information, please visit **www.businessexpertpress.com**, or contact **sales@businessexpertpress.com**.

www.ingramcontent.com/pod-product-compliance
Lightning Source LLC
Chambersburg PA
CBHW061831220326
41599CB00027B/5258